I0620211

LAW OF POSITION AND LOCATION

A POSITION THEORY

PHILOSOPHY

A REVISION

We take as given the idea of distinction and the idea of indication, that in order to make an indication one must first make a distinction. We take therefore the form of distinction for the form. G. Spencer-Brown, 1979, Laws of Form, 1.

LAW OF POSITION AND LOCATION
A POSITION THEORY

DELRIDGE LA VEON HUNTER, Ph. D MSCMH, CRC

PHILOSOPHY

A REVISION

We take as given the idea of distinction and the idea of indication, that in order to make an indication one must first make a distinction. We take therefore the form of distinction for the form. G. Spencer-Brown, 1979, Laws of Form, 1.

ARPress
ILLUMINATING IDEAS
EMPOWERING VOICES

Copyright © 2023 by Dr. Delridge Laveon Hunter

All rights reserved. No part of this publication may be reproduced, distributed, or transmitted in any form or by any means, including, photocopying,recording, or other electronic or mechanical methods, without the prior written permission of the copyright owner and the publisher, except in the case of brief quotations embodied in critical reviews and certain other noncommercial uses permitted by copyright law. For permission requests, write to the publisher, addressed "Attention: Permissions Coordinator," at the address below.

ARPress
45 Dan Road Suite 5
Canton MA 02021

Hotline:1(888) 821-0229
Fax:1(508) 545-7580

Ordering Information:
Quantity sales. Special discounts are available on quantity purchases by corporations, associations, and others. For details, contact the publisher at the address above.

Printed in the United States of America.

ISBN-13:	Paperback	979-8-89330-576-0
	eBook	979-8-89330-578-4
	Hardback	979-8-89330-577-7

Library of Congress Control Number: 2024900814

Law of Position and Location, A Position Theory

Abstract

The Law of Position and Location, a Position Theory, uses the premise of the Laws of Form as the basis of the numerous axioms that make up this paradigm. Each axiom contains a set of theorems that explain the rules of crossing, calling ((naming) and location (position) as operational forms within a polity of culture. Each axiom is layered to complement and support the others with axioms containing the rules that define distinction as an operational form of inequality. The two, operational processes here that explain the system are crossing and calling (naming). The position theory as a location theory, applies crossing and calling as indicators of the distance between the least favored and the most favored positions. The form of distinction as the original form establishes the motive for the creation of operational barriers to keep the other forms of distinction from crossing. To indicate what forms are to be distinguished from the original form, a name is to be attached to each form to inform that particular, what value is assigned to that name called. The name called and called again establishes that name as an indication of what form of distinction it is.

[Although Location is on the other side of position, location, the word, will not be used throughout this document. It will always implied that location us intended.]

A Time of Discovery

While employed as an Expediter, at the H. Singer Zone Center in Rockford, Illinois from 1966-1969 I was introduced to a new theoretical construct called "Position Theory." Position Theory, I was told, was never written down by the author, a well respected clinical social worker, but it was well known within his institution because he taught it to his graduate students. After learning how he applied the new construct, I found the name useful in understanding other definitions of social arrangements. It may be applicable to almost every thing constructed.

Position Theory immediately resolved the problematic with theoretical constructs based on race/color/class, nationality/religion/creed, and gender/gender relations. As I now understand the theoretical frame, Position Theory applies to anything that has itself as its own particular while operating as part of a whole. Position with its broad and deep connotations in usage is a simple equation that can operate on any level or with anything, i.e., it can apply to any form of distinction.

In listening to my informants it was immediately revealed how Position Theory may inform my effort to understand the competition in complementarities of an open society by adapting it to the study of social intercourse. Position Theory [location] as applied here is an integrated process that involves applying many fields of study or disciplines simultaneously as one. Prior to the development of integrative study more often than not research and instruction involved an examination of a piece of things or activities that happened in particular past, or after the fact, as a disciplinary, i.e., taken from the whole, a part/piece of) research or instructional procedure. No other ways of researching social forms was deemed legitimate: this is empiricism. This means of conducting research and instruction dominated university research for most of the 20th century. As we approach the first decade of the new millennium, the 21st century, the notion of disciplinary learning is no longer considered the only way of receiving a more focused understanding of behavior as it operates within the realm of social intercourse. [1996, C.E.]

The old process of dividing social intercourse into minute parts of study is now informed by integrating the focal points of complementary fields of inquiry. Offering a holistic view of any matter under discussion now complements disciplinary learning. Study in the realm of social intercourse that has developed within the polity of culture offers scholars a new way to examine the interaction between all of the other positions that exist as what I call the least and most favored positions in an open society.

A new paradigm is what the Position Theory has brought to the discussion on social constructs. It was in hearing the name Position Theory that allowed me to move beyond the old theoretical constructs I found wanting. The name position/location applies to anything and anybody, individual, group or any larger configuration thinkable that can be identified by calling the name. Creatively the Position Theory is like Blues, in that, it uses two processes: crossing and calling (naming and re-calling) to serve as the base of any observation made. Blues, the music of (from) Africa, allows any equation as a composition to be rendered simply by starting with three minor tones. Back during the late eighteenth and early nineteenth centuries, one could hear these minor tones played in Blues or any of the forms created out of that form of music.

With Blues serving as the analogy, here is a brief viewing of Position Theory as a working paradigm reflecting the manners or ways and means of Blues Aesthetics.

Position Theory maintains that to use crossing and calling as viable constructs permits scholars to inform their observations by realizing that crossing is a process operational when boundaries have been set and barriers erected. Either one crosses the barrier or one does not. A scholar may observe the activity-taking place as it is in motion during the movement to cross. An observation is made of the activity that is Omni-present and interactive. It allows one to study the position and the process.

Since the process of crossing is ongoing during this attempt to cross over, to learn the value of the crossing of one attempting to get over to the other side, one must know the name with a value attached to the crossing. As the challenge to the person seeking mobility, the crossing must possess a value equal to or greater than the name of the caller. Calling the name of the crossing, i.e., to go over to the other side, that has been named, gives value to the name called. It also shows the greater value assigned to the barrier erected to deny the crossing. The observations of crossing and calling are dynamic processes to be studied.

Social beings are always making adjustments with the knowledge that each has about movements in relationship to the information available about how and when to cross, if crossing is permissible. Crossing and calling have to do with the original mark of distinction made and barriers established by the entity that created the boundary. How a distinction is made and how the boundary is indicated to show a distinction is the role of language. The language that expresses the movement of entropy is what Position Theory allows one to investigate.

The likeness of Position Theory to Blues as a form of distinction is a demonstration of how the Position Theory may be used to inform scholars of what major contributions have been made directly by the least favored people. The information may be taken from the above statements regarding the minor tones. What has come out of the blues form of distinction is the invention of music the evolved into multiple sets that continued to expand. These new musical ideas all emanate from experiences working with three minor tones. The past creative activities are important contributions to the progression and development of world music. However, the contributions are virtually ignored by the dominant culture in the United States.

Applying the Position Theory, to the study of blues forms, allows scholars to see that the application of minor tones has resulted in the fundamental changes in modern music. This major contribution to music resulted from the creativity of the least favored people in society. Yet this music is not exemplified, as having any worth because the form of distinction casts on the contributors is that of the least favored position.

Correspondingly, that same music adapted by members of the most favored, i.e., George Gershwin, assume more currency simply because these contributors hold positions as members of the most favored in society. With the George Gershwin analogy, what crossing the boundary has shown is it was only when a member of the most favored found blues in the form of Jazz a musical construct that could inform his work that the music began to receive acknowledgement as an artistic form worthy of listening to, i.e., worthy of recognition. Prior to his intervention, any artistic form emanating from the least favored was denied any crossing, except as the primitive works of a buffoon.

New Thinking Has Emerged

The least favored and the most favored as positions, have allowed me to observe bias as an operational form within the United States and most other polities of culture. However, my design as constructed within the least favored and most favored positions only allowed an application of black and white positions taken from chess. In other words, my initial design outlined the black and white positions as least favored and most favored, but did not advance the notion into a new paradigm until crossing and calling were understood.

The desire was to create a new workable paradigm. There was a need for a new premise supported by axioms. The idea was to create sets in the form of axioms that would offer new ways of examining social intercourse. Now the task was to give new definitions and language to the process.

The design of the Position Theory is to allow scholars to delve into how bias serves as a motive to establish a boundary of distinction in an open society. Must there be a motive for bias to become the ideological form that promotes discrimination? Must there be the intent to harm a particular group for bias to operate? Must there be a motive for one group to name another group that already has a form of indication that it accepts as defining who it is? These are questions   pondered after reading chapter 1, Laws of Form. This is getting ahead of the story.

Moving to New York City in 1977 after spending a year in E. St. Louis, six years in Rockford, Illinois, and seven years in Ithaca, New York, I visited all of the bookstores I came across in Greenwich Village, until I happened upon a small intellectual bookstore located on Astor Place between Broadway and Lafayette. What attracted me to the store was the sight of men dressed in European cut suits standing with a book in their hands as they perused these works with great interest. At some point during my visits, I noticed, located on a shelf in the window of the bookstore was a new book entitled, Laws of Form. G. Spencer-Brown, a mathematician/philosopher who taught at Cambridge University, wrote it.

At first I simply stared through the window at the book every time I visited the bookstore and wondered, "Who would write a book on laws of form and call it logic?" I always concluded as I entered the store, "It looks very interesting." Yet, I never looked for it on the shelf for quite some time. Instead, I wandered through the works that I had wanted to examine. I did not want to get side tracked. Eventually, I went to the philosophy section to look for the work to no avail. Not finding it, I approached the person at the counter and said, "Good afternoon, excuse me. Under what section will I find Laws of Form by G. Spencer-Brown?"

I recalled a surprised look of disdain immediately expressed across his body. He said after a great pause, with the obvious disdain still present and never bothering to return the salutation, "Laws of Form can be found in philosophy or mathematics, we have it located in both categories because of the nature of the work," as he turned his body away from his customer. I responded, understanding the tone, the language, and the gesture, "I looked in the philosophy section and it was not there, that is why I came to you, to seek your assistance." He was embarrassed. His bad behavior was so obvious that other customers looked on in amazement as they looked at me to see my response. I smiled at his behavior, shook my head in disbelief, as I walked away from the counter.

I discovered the book in the mathematics section, and did what was custom, tore the cellophane cover away from the brand new book and began to read it. I discovered unlike the other esoteric works there, it was in paperback. Not waiting to read the biographic sketch of the author and/or the review on the back of the book, I began reading the preface. I read it once. I read it again and again until I fully understood what was said. "That was only the preface," I said. "God Damn, this is some heavy doo doo." This is after my first reading. I thought, "Wow, this is interesting and I have not even read the introduction, yet. I could not get past the preface. I had never seen anything like this before. "I've got to buy this book." The price was around $20.00. The book became chapter one. That chapter became my obsession. It became the book. I would recite "We take as given the idea of distinction and the idea of indication, that in order to make an indication one must first make a distinction. We take therefore the form of distinction for the form." "Heavy! Heavy!"

As a catechism, I recited that chapter and verse everyday until rote memory took hold of the concept, the design, and the logic of the two constructs. The dual constructs called crossing and calling became my obsession. The two work in tandem. It is now understood that the notion of how crossing the boundary that is erected to keep someone out allows me to understand what the idea of crossing means under a new construct: the other variable necessary as a protector to crossing is calling. Everything must be called something. Everybody seems to require a name to be recognized by. The name is the indication of how a particular form will be recognized upon being called. What names will that particular person or group be called?

Papers, proceedings, articles, books, etc., on the Position Theory have been delivered at conferences and other gatherings of intellectuals. No matter the forum, it all comes back to chapter one. It is chapter one that retains my attention for the next twenty odd years until I finally get it. All of the time spent pondering the Laws of Form my progress I share with my scholar learners in class. It is apparent that this sharing with my scholar learners over the school years has brought its rewards. The rewards come from having each class read the Laws of Form and the Position Theory and offer their own analyses of the constructs.

Writing the Law of Position/Location

At last, in 2002, I sat down at a Barnes and Nobel bookstore in Poughkeepsie, NY and wrote what became four axioms. The premise plus axioms are what have emerged as a Law of Position, a position theory. A set of questions inform my Law of Position as an explanation of social intercourse as an operational form within the polity of the culture called the United States of America. My basic query is what form of distinction assumed the original and most favored position in the United States prior to it becoming a State.

Questions were developed in 1977-78 while conducting research for my Ph. D. thesis, The Puritan Invention, in Economics of Education, Education Policy Analysis and Africana Studies at Cornell University. My research led me to the Puritans. It was in studying the Puritans Invention that I thought of the idea of a most favored position as a working model for my thesis. [In 1978/79, I read the entire contract of the Massachusetts Bay Colony in old English at the New York Research Library on 5th Avenue and 42nd Street.]

As I read the contract, it becomes apparent that the most favored position is occupied by the European Americans, in the forms of Dutch, French and British, who have established themselves as occupiers of the original and therefore most favored position in the New World Colony to be called "America." Again, in complementarities the slaves from Africa by design will become the occupiers of the least favored position. As it were, the African American will occupy the least favored position while the European American will occupy the most favored position. The Indigenous Peoples who were virtually exterminated remained in the least favored as "insignificant" Historical Others whose Names were to be abused as (a)historical figures (objects).

The forms of indication that will give credence to those forms of distinction as the names they will retain and/or assign themselves as the original and most favored names, e.g., Winthrop and assign to others regarded as not of and less than As a starter, the European American renames himself "White Man" and assumes the name "America" to the United States of America. White now becomes a favored position expressed as a color of Homo sapiens from Europe. The name America will become the abbreviation of the United States of America. That will become the most favored color to represent the people who are superior. He renames the African Negro and all others accordingly. Black becomes the least favored position as a color to represent the people so defined, i. e., inferior. The white man is the "American" while all others are to affix another name to America to indicate that they too are Americans. From the inception of the New World Colony of North America, it has been "America" at the expense of the other Americas: North, Central, and South, Latino, French, British, Indigenous, Asian, and African.

Out of those two questions (p. 6), the Law of Position, a position theory, has evolved. The intent by the use of the first chapter of Spencer-Brown's work is to form the construct as my premise. The purpose is to investigate the forms of distinction and the forms of indication as they may apply within an open society, e.g. North America.

Introduction

The Law of Position, a Position Theory takes its form from the rules of chess regarding the black position vs. the white position. As applied within this context the black occupies the least favored position while the white occupies the most favored. Any appearance of likeness to past or current theories of chess, race/color/class, gender/sex, religion/creed, and other theories as forms of discourse is only coincidental. However, these previously mentioned theories are "positions" that may serve to inform the process of enquiry. One may say that the rules of distinction and indication apply to all of the previously mentioned theories.

How it works is by employing the Law of Position, a position theory, one may consciously apply the rules distinction and indication to any form that shows by name there is an indication of a mark of distinction without having to use the exception rule in the process. The exception rule is applied when those who are formally left out of the process are now included because they are thought of as exceptions: their skill level permits them entry. But, heretofore, they had no privy to enter, the new ability to enter, by a few made them exceptions. They become the Important Men always treated in History. Thus, although the Constitution of the Hau-de-no-sau-nee Confederacy was read with great interest by many of the Founding Fathers, no mention is made of this reading.

The Law of Position does not explicitly intend nor by implication attempt to negate the theories previously stated. Position as used here means a person is according the rules (ideas) of distinction and indication occupy a location or as a location a position. The positions according to these rules emanate from the most and least favored position as applied to chess.

However, in using the Law of Position, one does not have to apply the exception rule to a particular, when that particular fits within a discussion of a construct under any of the above systems of analyses.

A Basic Premise

We take as given the idea of distinction and the idea of indication, that in order to make an indication one must first make a distinction. We take therefore the form of distinction for the form. G. Spencer-Brown, 1979, Laws of Form, 1.

Axiom 1

The crossing indicates the distinction of the boundary.

By drawing a boundary between each group as separate formations, one formation cannot reach the other formation without crossing the boundary that makes a distinction, i.e., when a boundary between groups is set up, one group cannot reach the other group without crossing the boundary that separates them.

Once a distinction is made for each formation, groups on each side of the boundary, being distinct can be identified as different. There can be no distinction of groups without motive. There can be no motive unless these groups are thought to differ in value. The group that holds the most favored form of distinction is considered to hold the most value. The intent and/or desire of the least favored groups are to cross the boundary into the position occupied by that group. The value assumed by the group wanting to cross indicates the greater value awarded to and assumed by the most favored group.

The group that holds the least favored form of distinction is considered to hold the least value. The intent and/or desire of the most favored group are not to cross the boundary into the position occupied by that group. The value assumed by the group not wanting to cross indicates the lesser value assigned to and imposed on the least favored group. For the least favored group who desires to enter the position of the most favored and then re-enter their own position, it is like they never entered the position of the most favored, at all.

No one from a group outside of the formation of the most favored position is permitted to enter their formation without approval from or by the most favored.

Groups not allowed to enter the position of the most favored are forbidden to enter the space of the most favored position. Forms of distinction are thereby indicated by positions assigned each competing, corresponding and complimentary group outside of the most favored position. Simply put, each group outside of the most favored position occupies a less favored position.

The extreme opposite group to the most favored is assigned and assumed to occupy the least favored position by those more favored.

Axiom 2

Words create the language of indication to describe the form of distinction.

It is through the usage of symbols called words that we establish language as a means of indication of the motive that brings about a form of distinction. It is through the usage of symbols called words that we call the name of each boundary created to separate one form of distinction from another. It is through the usage of words that a language is developed to give name to that form of distinction. It is through the usage of language that we establish how crossing a boundary of distinction is determined or when that crossing is permitted. It is the usage of language that the motive has a basis of expression for a form of distinction that is made. It is through the further usage of language that a distinction made is an indication of motive.

Put differently, a group thus indicated by an expression of the name is also an indication of the value assigned to that group as a form of distinction.

Axiom 3

The distinction of the claim is indicated by the name.

When a particular group is considered the most favored, i.e., the group that occupies the most favored position of distinction among groups, the name the most favored group assumes, can be taken to indicate the value of the group because of the position of distinction it occupies. To assign a particular group value greater than others, different names can be taken to indicate the value of each of the groups so assigned. To call a group by the name assigned or assumed indicates the value of the distinction enjoyed the group so named. To use that name to call the group again means the value is seen in the name called. The value assigned establishes a distinction that is indicated by the name called. The intent of those who occupy the most favored position is to limit those allowed and/or forbidden to use their name because that name is an indication of their more favored position as a form of distinction. Equally, when the name of the group is indicated to express the value of the group the form of distinction is indicated by the name.

In other words, the name is an indication of the degree of value derived by and/or assigned to that form of distinction.

Axiom 4

Principle as an Operational Form Of Distinction
The Inequality Distinction is an Indication of a Form of Inequality

A reminder: We take as given the idea of distinction and the idea of indication and in order to make an indication we must first draw a distinction. We take therefore the form of distinction for the form.

We take as given that the original form of distinction is the first form. Any other form of distinction created after the original form that is not of or from the original form is unequal in value to the original form. We take therefore the original form of distinction as the form that occupies the most favored position with the most value attributed to that position.

Once the first form of distinction has been established and is accepted as the original and most favored position with a boundary surrounding it, a new form with a boundary is established as a separate form of distinction. The boundary of the new form establishes a position of inequality between forms.

What we are contending here is, to create a form of distinction we must establish a boundary that separates the original as the first form of distinction from any other forms of distinction created thereafter. Once a boundary is established between these forms of distinction an inequality of value is assumed to exist between forms.

For a distinction of inequality to be made between each form a name is given to each [form] as a means of indication as to which [form] holds what distinction that is of more or less value than others. That is, for the original form of distinction to be considered different and of greater value because of its originality, for any other form, a name is assigned to indicate the value of that particular form. The value assigned to each form of distinction is indicated by the name chosen to distinguish that form from other forms. Once a value has been designated to each form by name, the name indicates the distinction in value attributed to that form so named. There must be a motive for one occupying the original position to offer names to other forms not considered part of the original form of distinction or of equal value thereof. Once a name is chosen to indicate one form is of greater value than another a motive has been established. A motive to distinguish one form from another by name establishes an assumption of inequality between forms. Once a motive has been established, value assigned each form by the name called indicates that there is an assumed inequality between forms. In other words, all forms of equal distinction carry the same name.

A difference of name assumes that there is difference of form. That difference of form the distinction is indicated by the name given that form. Stated differently, an unequal value is attached to the name as a description of the form whereby difference establishes one called by that name a position that is less favored. This is called a position of inequality, i.e., a less favored position. When a name identifies each member as an equal within the form, i. e., each member has the same access as a possibility. Any additional name assigned to any member indicates that within the form the additional name has a different value assigned.

When different value assigned to a name is of less value than a more favored name a less favored position is established. Here greater access serves as the means of receiving a chance to advance ones position: a lesser degree of access offer less chances or opportunities to advance from a lesser position. This lack of access establishes a dialogical process of denial and non-recognition.

The lesser form of distinction offers less advantage of opportunity to that so indicated. Put differently, those with the greater degree of access receive a greater chance to advance their position, while those with lesser degree of access receive less chance to advance their or out of their position. In an open system whereby fluidity is operational, it is the degree of openness practiced within process that allows fluidity to provide the Least Favored access beyond that offered through fair practices of Affirmative Action.

Where unequal beings of consciousness exist, an inequality of position within the theatre of social intercourse is indicated by the names assigned.

Axiom 5
The Rule of Negation

The Negation Rule is designed to disallow the least favored any advancement of its position. It is also to disallow any advancement out of that position. The rule is to deny the movement of the least favored into any more favorable positions. It is to make the attempt at upward mobility ineffective if not invalid. The intent is to break the complementarities' of positions that enrage efforts to allow those who occupy the least favored position any way to create growth and development toward re-inventing themselves as a means of up mobility. Put differently, it is this denial of movement out of the least favored position. Thus, the mark of distinction in this instance allows the negation rule to deny the least favored from crossing the barrier. The inability to cross the barrier allows the naming and the calling of the name to place stigmas on the ones so named, e.g., Negro, Gypsies (Roma People), American Indians (Indigenous People of the Americas). Ad infinite

Naming (Inclusive)

The African renames Negro is used as an example of a process of negation by assigning a mark of distinction might be located and named to indicate who/what might be identified as people in bondage .
This is a case of the process operating.
Invention of the Negro
The Process

1. People Trafficking

The process of the invention of the Negro began with the People Trafficking of Africans from particular locations that supplied the workers necessary to perform the types of labor required to develop the agriculture, industrial and trade economy at that particular phase of economic development. The man stealing took place within these villages because they housed the types of workers who were needed to perform specific labor tasks. The labor tasks required dictated the skills sought out by the slavers. To steal people arbitrarily or on a whim was too inefficient and costly. So time was spent locating the "tribe" that performed the labor required developing the agricultural, industrial or trade economy.

2. Transporting

The process of the invention of the Negro moved to the second stage with the transportation of the African to the newly named colonized Americas.

3. Processing – Naming

The process of the invention of the Negro moved to the third stage by processing the African as a Negro into the system of bondage with the old Generic name being replaced by a new name, Negro. As the Negro, the people of the old continent no longer have a place of origin that is clearly defined, i.e., there is no Negro Land.

4. Locating

The process of the invention of the Negro moved to the forth stage with location of the African as a Negro into a colonial place, e.g. New Amsterdam, and living – work space now about to be given the new "Christian" name as an indentured servant.

5. Renaming—A new name for the African person, so-called Negro, a Christian name is the slave's name

The process of the invention of the Negro moved to the fifth stage with the renaming—naming of the Negro as (s) he is given a Christian first name that is to be certified as the official name of that slave.

6. Indenturing (position servitude)

The process of the invention of the Negro moved to the sixth stage with process of servitude being offered as a permanent position of the worker. The name indicates the position the name implies.

7. Enslaving

The process of the invention of the Negro moved to the seventh stage with the name Negro meaning slave and the Christian name meaning that is how that particular slave it be identified.

8. Enforcing

The process of the invention of the Negro moved to the eighth stage within the boundary being that of a slave established as the holder of the least favored position by law, with the name Negro indicating the boundary that serves to distinguish itself from the others.

The American Indian Construct

The American Indian construct uses that name of a people not thought to have any advancement worthy of being called by their names because they have no civilization. Not knowing that not all people want to live the way they live, and where India is or who the Indians are the name are the only one the European explorers knew to call any people thought to be where they think they are. Later American is added to assure everyone just learning about these people that they are some-place-else. The new information informs everyone that they were located in the Americas not Asia as previously imagined. Never acknowledging that these European voyagers did not know where they were in space and time, they would never state that these people are given the wrong name. They are given names of another people thousands of miles away. The notion is that they are going to keep that name because like the use of the word Negro the name according to C.L.R. James, serves a "commercial" purpose. People from another place should not be disadvantaged by having to learn every name of every ethnic group called "a tribe". As with the name Indian, the name tribe comes from within the European names of what they are at a different point in socio-cultural development. Likening the Indigenous communities to an understanding of how they developed, these people are thought to be at the "primitive" state of development. Thus, treatment of these communities is thought to worthy of the disadvantages placed upon them. Oppression is thought to be commiserate what mark of distinction is applied this group, so named. They are the least favored in the land mass just assumed to be their own decided these rules created under the Doctrine of Discovery or what the Americans call a state's "Manifest Destiny" give the most favored the Privileges and Immunity take and do what they want. For, they are founding a "new world 5has become the America Delrina.

Examples of other names with a Mark of Distinction that are Indicated by these names: tribe, woman, white, black, savage, nigger, fag, dike, Mexican, Spanish, Bi-polar, rifer, ad finite...

Axiom 6
The Privileges and Immunity Clause of the 14th Amendment

The U.S. Constitution states, "No State shall make or enforce any law which shall abridge the privileges or immunities of citizens of the United States." By de facto use of (inclusive) this clause of the 14th Amendment written to protect the civil rights of the African American and others has been diverted to offer privileges and immunities to the least favored population that are called " po' white trash, Irish, Spic" etc., under the race construct.

Axiom 7
Catalyst
Location/production/process

A Catalyst offers, supplies, provides, makes possible, the means, the channel, the vehicle, the method, the medium, the mechanism, the access, to crossing the barrier.

Axiom 8
The Fairness Principle [The Catalyst Construct}

An operational form called affirmative action of the three (3) clauses of the 14th Amendment of the U.S. Constitution.

Under the fairness principle in a system whereby all social intercourse is equal, goods and services are offered at a fair market value. In a market system, it is in games, e.g., baseball, basketball, etc., that fairness may be practiced in its most objective form. Outside of games, fairness assumes that all goods, services and other forms of social intercourse are available to each according to the value held within the market place of supply and demand. Thus, it is only in games that fairness expresses a measure of merit. In other practices of social intercourse, fairness is awarded according to what position one holds. It, therefore, serves as an operational process of inequality between positions. In so doing the social interaction of it supersedes the ability to establish a "level playing field." In current society, that is called Affirmative Action.

Affirmative Action serves as the ways and means of providing access by establishing a process that offers equal opportunity to the least favored under the fairness principle. The motive is to establish a "level playing field," i.e., offering the least favored access to those areas and materials formally denied. In an effort to establish a level playing field access is provided to the Least Favored in the arenas of employment, housing, entertainment, play, education, the arts, civic life, and other ways and means of conducting social intercourse. Affirmative Action becomes the mode and means of measuring quantitatively the actual success rate, i.e., rate of return, of fairness as a practice within a society that employs two forms of distinction: The most and least favored.

With forms of distinction serving as a way of separating those who are most favored from those who are the least favored, equal opportunity moves the least favored no further away from their original position than before. Except for a change in the social order of inequality sustained by bias, fairness cannot be realized applying Affirmative Action as at means to better access through equal opportunity to all citizens (inclusive) of a given jurisdiction.

Affirmative Action operating within the confines of positions of favor, only permits fairness with a definable demonstrated outcome (DDO), e.g., baseball score of 5 to 4, when the process is conducted as games (a play activity) based on quantitative measurements. As an analogy to civil life, measurement on a quantitative level, Affirmative Action offers no quantitative or qualitative changes to show for its effort. There is no objective change in who occupies the least favored. Despite no meaningful change realized by the least favored, opposition to that effort has led the opponents to allege a false premise called reverse discrimination. Reverse discrimination presupposes that those at the bottom of the social scale once given the opportunity to advance will help the neighbors too, so?

A use of reverse discrimination by the least favored becomes a negation of the negation: Only the most favored can engage in reverse discrimination. That is what we call Affirmative Action. Reverse discrimination by the least favored becomes a reversal of the illusive forward movement the least favored have made on their own. Reverse discrimination supposes the power relationship to authority is one whereby the least favored now has power equal to that held by the most favored. That certainly is not how things are.

What the opposition is bringing to light is the appearance of unity among the least favored. Unity is not reverse discrimination. No matter, unity of the least favored is challenged as cheating, a violation of Affirmative Action thus undemocratic, as showing favoritism to members within the group. On the other hand the most favored is expected to choose from within their ranks for upward movement. It is they who must provide open access as a process for Affirmative Action to increase the value of those less favored. Even so, providing access to those previously denied can never completely reverse the discrimination suffered by these groups, as the least favored.

Put differently, the least favored are not in a position to engage in a practice reserved for the most favored: that of allowing an unequal distinction to be made between equals under the law. In effect the socially based, politically enacted inequality practices are not disturbed without a transformation of the market system regardless of allegations to the contrary.

To camouflage denial emanating through bias practice, a process called purchasing power parity (PPP) is offered as a way for creating a virtually level play field. In reality the whole notion of creating a mathematical economic formula for calculating parity as virtual when there is no value change, only sustains the inequality principle between positions involving social intercourse. What PPP does is offer an explanation of the vast differences between the two positions that is in a language understandable to the most favored. [This fore stated narrative can be found in the book, "Culture of Whiteness VS Black Popular Culture: a Law of Position" Amazon Books]

After Thought
Calling and Crossing

What I found interesting in my examination of Laws of Form was how easy it was to label others as exhibiting some disability or disadvantage, e. g., hair or skin color, that allowed them to be grouped with others for discriminatory purposes of who appears to exhibit the same disability or disadvantage. A disability in this instance is something someone else defines as have a displeasing (disabling) appearance (inclusive) thus placing him or her as a disadvantaged. The disabling appearance as a form of distinction identified is indicated by the name called. By calling those so identified with that name is designed to express the intent of the label, e. g., Negro meaning, from Africa, occupier of the least favored position, i.e., the black position, as in chess. Location as a Position allows calling one Negro, the Latin word for Black in English, to assume the name to be negative. The name makes the Negro, the person, undesirable, i. e., the negation rule.

The motive for creating such a label is to discriminate against the group so named. Calling the name of those thought deserving of this form of distinction is done so as to identify to the greater community how such groups should be recognized when their name is called.

The intent of calling a group that is less favored by a name that carries disparaging results is to establish a barrier of entrance to the group so named. On the other side of the equation is the response of members of the group disparaged is to violate the rule, by crossing, the barrier of exclusion. Please recall, in an open society there are always stated rules of entrance and rejection. To overcome rejection, these ways and means of entrance are learned. Thus when a member of group disparaged happens to find ways of crossing the barrier they apply the rules and when successful they enter the new position by the ways and means they learned.

At this point, if entrance sought is not approved of, but serve as no deterrence to the upward mobility, other barriers are erected or set into place to limit entrance to only those things identified as permissible by the more favored groups. Engaging in the search for further entrance additional ways and means are sought out and applied. There are those who succeed, e.g., Miles Davis and Madam Walker, while others have failed, e.g., Mike Tyson. In other words, the less favored must thus find other avenues of crossing barriers that constantly appear as the next barrier – called hurdle – to over come.

The intent of erecting further barriers is to never allow, i.e., deny, that member of the least favored to gain enough favors to become a member of the particular most favored group, e.g., as in the case of Princeton University denying Paul Robeson entrance although he graduated Valedictorian of his Princeton High School graduating class. He was admitted to Rutgers, the State University of New Jersey, also a land-grant college. As things happen the least favored university in regard to Princeton was the recipient of a product of the least favored who surpassed the standards necessary for admittance into European culture, yet was denied entrance by the most favored.

For upward mobility in an open society to be realized, there appears to be a design, e.g., entrance to and graduation from a prestigious institution, a desire to enter and availability. Without access, fairness and merit there is less likelihood for admittance to operate in favor of the least favored as a group, e.g., Nina Simone, was denied entrance the famous music conservatory in Philadelphia. Some members of the least favored positions are allowed to cross the barrier erected to deny entrance based on the admission standard of that group, e.g., Collin Powell and Condoleezza Rice.

In other words, those allowed to cross the barrier are declared "qualified" members from the least favored. Stated differently, the possibilities of the removal of barriers that appear before a member of the least favored are nil to minuscule thus allowing only a selected few entrance. Further, entrance may be temporary as many have discovered after they have returned to their old positions e.g., many Rhythm and Blues/Rock and Roll "stars" fell from fame after a brief stay in the music business. A return to the old position is like never entering the new position.

Permanence is only realized when the offspring of the former members of the least favored group are accepted as members by those whose acceptance is considered representing the authority of group entrance. With this in mind, many families of least favored parents devote a life time prep their children to leave their old position, enter a new more advanced position and make allowances so that their offspring will remain there or advance further. These parents are willing to pay the opportunity costs to see their children are invested in as human capital. Epoch discourages or at least minimizes any notions of fairness; access and equality of opportunity that moves those currently in the most favored positions into positions lower than one they currently occupy. Thus relative expansion with proper investments assure the scholar learner invested in will be able to move into a better way of life than that enjoyed by the family at the moment. That idea is only doable in an open society.

What this dialectic or dialogic represents is its contradictions inherent in an open society based on what is required for the most favored to maintain social control. Looking at the current dynamic, the social arrangement of this of the number of members allowed into new more favored positions is one way of keeping its membership current and fluid.

THE END

DIALOGUES

ALIENATION
DELRIDGE LA VEON HUNTER

(READ ALOUD)

Characters

Miles

Nefarati

Ida B.

Tell The Truth

Signify

Nos Everything

Tanesha

Ray

Mind Boggled

Singer

Streams of Consciousness Choir

Diction Arian

Alienation is a feeling of estrangement from ones community and self. In this instance one feels a sense of powerlessness in that there is no control over what one is able to do within the confines of the current definition of being. Having no power over how one` will reach ones potential another feeling of being able to offer no meaningful contribution to the development and advancement of self creates a distance between the external world and the internal consciousness of becoming. Once alienation has become embedded within its own psychology isolation sets in as a means of creating a distance between the self and other. A feeling of nothingness occurs when this alienation reaches a chronic state that encourages the personality to project behavior that appears anti-social and abnormal. Once this process has evolved to this point, the person exhibiting this behavior shows signs of defeat that makes that individual appear, helpless, without thought, without culture and without self worth.

[The statement above is said to the audience. The players never hear it. A state of oppression and the habitually minor character of its tones may well be ascribed to the depression of feeling, the anguish that must forever fill the heart of those who are forced to lead a life so fraught with woe. This is clearly exemplified as the sad story of this musical race comprehensively told below…]

Miles
You are talking about Invisible Man by Ralph Ellison aren't you Dictionarian?

Nefatari
Or, it might just as easily be Richard Wright and Native Son, or, any number of novels from that period. Alienation was the theme that rang supreme. [In jest} I'm the poet and don't you know it?

Miles

[Smile] I hear yea. {Sarcasm}, yea right. [Now serious] Where unequal beings of consciousness exist, an inequality of position within the theatre of social intercourse is indicated by the names assigned.

Nefatari

Uh, huh!

Miles

[Pause] Yes, but my problem is, Black male alienation to the point of committing error of judgment characterized by the great novels that used the African American male as the feature failure proto-type male has always left me angry, very angry.

Signify

You mean pissed off, don't you Miles? That would make me pissed off like a dog.

Nefatari

Why were you so angry, Miles? What did these novels to you to make you so angry?

Miles

Each character comes out of the subconscious of Fraud. Each comes from a Eurocentric construct that seemed flawed.

Nefatari

The African American characters are wedded to the psychoanalysis of Fraud? Is that your objection?

Miles

Yes, they appeared to be a strangle hold on the Negro construct as examined by European American disciples of Fraud.

Nefatari

Are you referring to Mark of Oppression, American Dilemma? Works of that nature? But the two personalities you are referencing written by African American writers, one from Missouri, the other from Oklahoma. They are from the mid-west on the southern side, if you know what I mean.

Miles

Yes, but by authors who are not European American? I never think of those books, but I guess you have a point there. These are the works most influential about the pathologies of the so-called Negro. These pathologies are a result of "Racism."

Nefatari

You are referring to bias I take it? You are using Racism as a name of a particular bias, Is that what you are doing, Miles? Are you alleging that there is such a bias called Racism?

Miles

Yes, but my problem is with the assumption of that this dysfunctional Negro can never make the right existential decision about his life. He always makes the wrong decision.

Nefatari

Are you telling me that these authors are feeding the stereo-type of the African American male? Is that your position?

15

Miles

Yes, I guess that could be heard in the tone of my response. I can see the European American novelist saying African American males have the pathologies because it is in his best interest to put this propaganda forward. [Pause] But, to have someone who comes from the least favored position making the same allegation is a puzzle to me. These dudes studied Marx, too.

Nefatari

Why is it a puzzle when a novelist who happens to be from the least favored position writes a novel you expect from some one else? Are you accusing them of forgetting their dialectics?

Miles

Well, they are feeding the stereo-type that they are writing to disprove.

Nefatari

How are they feeding the stereo-type?

Mile

They are doing so by reinforcing everything negative about the Negro before he becomes African American.

Nefatari:

What examples do you have of these practices by the novelists you are speaking of?

Miles

"Native Son" by Richard Wright and "Invisible Man" by Ralph Ellison. I had great difficulty finishing these novels because their endings were so tragic. You could tell the ending as soon as you got into the novel.

Nefatari

Why do you suppose they did that?

Miles

They are trying to talk to the European Americans sensibilities and sense of shame.

Nefatari

They are trying to create a sense of moral suasion? Is that your point?

Miles

Yes, each seemingly wants to reach the hearts and minds of good thinking people about the plight of the African American male.

Nefatari

Something like the Sorrow Songs?

[Singing a sorrow song.]

SOCC:

…the habitually minor character of its tones may well be ascribed to the depression of feeling, the anguish that must ever fill the heart of those who are forced to lead a life so fraught with woe.

Miles

Yes, I never thought about that. Sorrow Songs, how about that?

Nefatari

So, what is your critique of these novels, and why are they so prominent?

Miles

That seems to have been the genre the publishers wants the public to read.

Nefatari

Why do you say that?

Miles

Because I never see any novels that do not paint a picture of negation about us.

Nefatari

So you think that the novels treat the black as an alienated group is only one sided?

Miles

Very!

Nefatari

Would you prefer a love story or a thriller with a hero as the main character?

Miles

That's not a bad idea. I never thought about that.

Nefatari

You want to see a thriller or mystery?

Miles: Well, I like to read something that comes out of our gift to the development of American English. We do have that facility.

Nefatari

Oh, that is original. I never think about the least favored people contributing to the lexicon of American English.

Miles

The African experience is unusual and original. There is much to develop novels from.

Tell the Truth

We did not trust our facility with language. We could not believe that the southern bred brothers and sisters had what it takes to copy from.

Nefatari

So you are taking sides with Zora Neale and Dunbar and Hughes to name a few.

Miles

Yes, we have no need to develop the European constructs to writing.

Nefatari

Okay, back to the novels of alienation of the black, what gave them their appeal to the general public, those that read?

Miles

The appeal was primarily fo the so-called "liberals." They got their groove off by, reading about the suffering of the disfranchised Negro in the United States It made them feel guilty about their plight.

Nefatari

Aren't you being kind of mean?

Miles

Mean? Please remember this was a time of terror of African Americans in the United States.

Nefatari

You are speaking about the lynching I take it?

Miles

Yes, the reasons to "kill a nigger hire another, kill a mule buy another" were omnipresent. Matter of fact you didn't need a reason. The only reason one required was desire to have one dead.

Nefatari

So your position is?

Miles

Lynching was licensed activity that was called a "picnic."

Nefatari

Picnic?

Miles

Yea, "pick a nigger, anyone will do. We can think of a reason after we kill the bastard. A dead nigger is a good nigger."

Nefatari

Or is it, a good nigger is a dead nigger.."

Miles

Whatever! So African Americans are oppressed and the novelists reinforce the psychology of that oppression by creating fictional characters that play out that oppression with their own pathologies.

Nefatari

You mean that the Negro is his own worst enemy? He himself is at fault?

Miles

All the Negro needs to do is to accept his plight, I should say her plight, with dignity and a humble demeanor.

Nefatari

You mean grin and bare it.

Miles

Yes 'um Miss Ne-fa-ta-ri, that's what I's mean. You sho' know yo' niggers, well.

Nefatari

Are you alleging that the alienation was self imposed?

Miles

Oh, that is exactly what the power elite or ruling class wants everybody around the world to believe. After all, are in "America" land of the free and the brave.

Singer

God bless America, land that I love.

Miles

Fear is everywhere. It is truly a dictatorial state. It is a time when the terror of the culture of whiteness reign supreme.

Nefatari

You are speaking of the south aren't you? It is the south that practiced this terror?

Miles

If, you call Nevada, Arizona, Indiana, New York, Ohio and other places "up south" the south then I guess you are right.

Singer

Lawd, Lawd, Lawd, Lawd, I ain't gon' tak dis place no mo.

Nefatari

Sounds like the novelists, as members of the least favored people, have no choice. Alienation is the only thing that is apparent. Writers tend to write about what is apparent. Alienation is the most pressing thing that oppression brought on. Most people are alienated during the period you are referring to. The Indigenous people are even more alienated. Women are alienated. Chinese people are alienated. And the otherly able are home ridden. Times are had for most of us.

Miles

Yes, that is true, but the Jazz musicians do not....

Nefatari

...Oh, be careful here. Remember the drug scourge that kills all of those Be Bop musicians? That appears to be alienation in its most extreme state. They act out their oppression just as the characters do in the novels with the only difference being the Jazz Musicians are doing their thing live while performing before an audience. The look great on stage, but...

Miles

Yes, you are so right. The novels are simply reflections of real life. They are the invisible native sons that the European Americans copy their forms from. We call them the least favored people in society. According to Ellison construct the invisible man is a total negation construct.

Nefatari

What do you mean, Miles? [Pause] I guess, the point would be, why not make one of the characters a Jazz musician? They are the creative examples of what alienation can create. Yes, the main character needs to be a Jazz musician who moves underground.

Signify

…And, people will walk by and hear him playing some where far away doing the days and he will play up top in the night.

Miles

Yes, he did. I mean he didn't but he did without the instrument. But self destruction while creating a new musical art form and aesthetic parade is worse, or what Mao calls a principle contradiction, to act out your oppression by self inflicted drug abuse while you invent the most beautiful music possible every night through improvisation, or to kill the patron who wants to see you perform music never heard before while you commit suicide in the process?

Signify

The contradiction for the Jazz musician is an apparent genius that is recognized on stage at the theatre but falls on deep shadows when walking the streets of the city.

Nefatari

[Goes into hood speak] That's some deep shit, Signify that was good. [Pause] [Back to intellectualism] So, according to Ellison, the least favored has two contradictions. What are they? These creative geniuses are visible while they perform on stage and invisible beings when they walk the streets coming to and going from work? Is that your position? Once they leave the stage?

`Signify

The native son is invisible to everyone who is in more favored positions on the out side. They are the ones who convict the alienated soul, the invisible native son. The Invisible Native Son is a blur to those passing in the street or on the sidewalk where all people meet.

Nos Everything

A crime of a too frighten creature, he bungles in his desire to keep the girl quiet.

Tanesha

In the film he looks like a petrified buffoon who cannot work his way out of a pillow case with his arms unimpeded. You want to strangle him for being so dumb. I mean dumb. You know "dis Nigga gon' hang." For show!

Nefatari

You seem to be making the point that the characters seem to be so fatalistic not even a supporter can defend them.

Signify

Not even one of them do good lawyers can save his ass. He dead!

Miles

I could not have said it better. It made me start to think? Am I that character?

Signify

His lack of being himself is so dire you wonder how he lives as long as he does? One would think that nothing but this level of negation would be a possible ending given a book.

Miles

Yes but you can see his struggle is one of ignorance, an ignorance of the tenth degree. It is just that bad. Never once is he given a book to read. His script has been written out from beginning to end. Except for the accidental killing invisible native son will never be heard of.

Nefatari

Funny thing is, the process appears to be rigged. His only fame will be infamy thus further negating this invisible native son as a worthy person everyone wants to have as a neighbor.

Signify

You know, [Pause] it is this powerlessness that rubs me the wrong way. I don't care about the neighbor. I prefer living in the country anyway, don't need no neighbors.

Nefatari

No neighbors Signify? What if you have an emergency? Just teasing! So what about this powerlessness?

Signify

Well it means I must act out to be heard. No other way will my voice be heard? It means I gotta kill somebody to be noticed. And that somebody must be the people they call white. Then somebody will pay me some attention. My escape from alienation is now satisfied. 'Cause somebody is going to listen to me.

Miles

Yes, but it means sudden death.

Nefatari

Well according to Orlando Patterson the alienated as a slave already suffers a social death. According to his analysis, a sudden death would not move you one spec off of the spot you are currently standing on. So what? Just anther dead person from the least favored position. It means nothing.

Signify

Orlando Patterson? He may have, but, I am discussing powerlessness which means I am not socially dead. [Back to Miles statement that set everybody on this journey] It defeats the purpose of the act to be killed immediately after the crime because there will be no story to tell afterwards. There must be a story to tell. I agree. A sudden death is definitely anti-climactic and counter- productive. A crime of an unpremeditated nature would have to happen because the perpetuator has lost his cool, had a panic attack, and goes crazy. But that is not my concern. My point is, I want the power invested in me spiritually to have the ability to have my songs performed and I receive the royalties these songs should provide.

[Everybody stop what they are doing and look at Signify.]

Miles

Signify, I did not know that you write songs. That you are a composer?

Everybody

Me either/neither! Ain't that nothing?

Nos Everything

I knowed it!

Miles

Yea right!

Signify

Yes, she's right. She's the only one who did. Nos Everything is the only one who believed in my work.

Miles

So when are we going to hear some of these tones. What genre is it, R&B, Hip Hop, Soul?

Signify

No, Jazz I write lyrics and score.

Tanesha

No stanking?

[Everybody crack up over Tanesha using a substitute for the S…word.]

HA!HA!HA!AHH!HA!HA!>>>>

Signify

You see, my point is, when we talk about alienation I think of the Jazz musicians are or use to be the most alienated artist….

Nefatari

….that includes painters, sculptors, actors and dancers.

Signify

Yes, you are right Nefatari. You are exactly right. We are among the most alienated creative people in the country.

Miles

Does that mean alienation is a code word for what Nefatari calls bias?

Ida B

I know we can spend time dissecting the construct of powerlessness, but this alienation discussion opens the door for other elements that make alienation a total process when it comes to keeping the defeated off the playing field.

Miles

Oh, I agree. There are many other components that work as alienating forms but…

Ida B

Sorry to cut you off Miles. Since Signify raised the powerlessness rule as a disincentive. And he's correct about that. However, I think there are other rules of alienation.

Nefatari

What rules are those, Ida B?

Ida B

The one I shall mention now is hopelessness.

Nefatari

Hopelessness? Now where does hopelessness fit into the invisible native son duel construct?

Ida B

Hopelessness is how alienation begins.

Miles

Um hum! Tell me more.

Ida B

Hopelessness sets in when recognition is withheld…

Nefatari

…and denial is used as the subterfuge.

Signify
Give an example?

Ida B

Hopelessness! Hopelessness is when the invisible native son sees no way out of the particular he is in. Seeing no way out is magnified by a job he has taken that he wished he had not taken. This is further magnified by him being forced against his internal will to take the most favored people to a night club in his community he has not been able to afford. Having no power, the invisible native son fails to keep his employers children from getting too drunk and becoming totally dependant on him. The problem is, the invisible native son is too ignorant to make a decision. He has been granted no tools of intellect. That makes him totally helpless, and otherwise invisible.

Tanesha

Speaking of the invisible, this is not how Ralph Ellison employed the use of the word. For Ellison the invisible native son is a very complex character who as a figure never reveals his true self to anyone. As the infamous narrator he hides behind the tools of language. For his college he is the politically correct rising colored student. For the trustees he is the handy man who can oblige their every need from delivering a rousing speech to the trustees to fighting his school mates with blinders on to satisfy their sadistic urges to see pain and make him demonstrate as the least favored who is made to fight like roosters and dogs. For the Brotherhood he can deliver a rousing speech despite efforts on their part to make his speeches to the community impossible. For Ras he is the enemy working for the white man. To the people the narrator in disguise is a ladies man, a numbers runner, a pimp and other lumpen activities reserved for that type of personality.

Nefatari

So how do you see the invisible nature of the narrator of the story?

Ida B

The narrator is both a character and a storyteller. His invisibility is a creation of his imagination yet he fools everybody else in the process.

Nefatari

Yes, but how does that make the character in the novel helpless? I'd call the narrator conniving, but helpless I fail to see that in his behavior.

Ida B

Oh, I beg to differ. Narrator is not powerless as you can see all of the ways he fools everybody like a camellia. Yet, he is helpless to help himself move beyond what others see him. He does and does not see that he is his biggest problem. He sets himself up....

Signify

...too fail?

Ida B

No! ...to continue the process he falls into on his journey.

Miles

Journey?

Tanesha

Journey where?

Ida B

We don't know. We never find out. Narrator never tells us. He simply takes on a new personality ride to show all of the skills he has. He lets us know that narrator is a very bright man. He graduates val. He wins a scholarship that is turned on its head and becomes his albatross. Yet, he has all of these skills. [Pause] Except for these demonstrations, these skills are only known to those privy to see a particular, no more, no less, only that particular....

Tanesha

...skill. do you mean a particular skill?

Ida B

No, I leave it at particular because that is how narrator presents his dream nightmare. He seems to be struggling with who he is and what his mission is here.

Signify

Is that his existential question?

Miles

He never finds it!

Nefatari

He never finds either or any, yet he demonstrates them all.

Tanesha

Ain't that, nothing?....

Ida B

So Professor Ellison creates a character who narrates his on terror as he moves from one imposition to another and another.

Miles

You know, thinking about it, this man is obsessed with Jazz as an aesthetic. Matter of fact, in Shadow and Art, he gives us our first look at how aesthetics is created. He uses the blues form jazz to demonstrate what the role of an aficionado is as a patron of this art music we lovingly call JAZZZ>

Signify

That is so true. Back to the main event the invisible native son, Ellison's version.

Nefatari

And, what is his conclusion as a sciz-o-tic character?

Tanesha

Girl did you just come up with a new word? What did the narrator conclude as a seiz-o-tic creature?

Ida B

The Narrator as character back door-ed down a man hole for life. At his pleasure he has 1000 light bulbs that are contributing to the ecological doom we are promised as he finally has the last laugh on capitalism. He is a communist with a little c. He is living free of rent, no utilities, all of the electricity he desires, plus he is totally invisible to those people who are crazy enough to live above ground for the rest of their lives.

Miles

He never comes above ground?

Ida B

Oh, he's above ground every night when the lights are bright. But nobody see him, pays any attention to his movements because to them he no longer exist. At least, not the character they know.

Nunez

You know I know this is off the point, but I gotta say it.

Nefatari

No, go ahead, what is it?

Nunez

Invisible native son should have been the character of a Jazz Man, a Jazz musician. Don't you think? Don't yawl think that the character should have been a Jazz musician?

Tanesha

This should bring us back to the existential question we were discussing about alienation.

Miles

Well, clearly the two characters which we made in an integrated construct with two particulars. A character we call the Invisible Native Son.

Nefatari

And what ere those particulars?

Miles

They are powerlessness and helplessness.

Signify

As represented by native son and invisible man!

Miles

One more thing about the original form novel, obviously he is of the opinion that blues offers the writer a different way to express a narrative form. I have always wondered what took him so long.

Nefatari

Oh, you are forgetting, he is learning Be Bop along with everybody else. How would you expect him to advance his new craft more quickly than those who are trying to learn how to play it on a horn, when it is the horn that is informing the process???

Miles

I could not have said it better. Ellison accident-ed upon something original, and, it came out of music, the new music of improvisation. It's the ability to improvise that Ellison never mastered as a horn player, but he can be so as a writer.

Nefatari

Interesting how he continues to second guesses his intuition. That may have been his error, why it takes him so long. He can never finish his solos. He is a John Coltrane as the novelist. I see this more so after reading Juneteenth. His solos never end.

Tanesha

So what about Richard? Richard Wright?

Miles

First I must acknowledge how bright and gifted these two writers were and how they made up the black intelligentsia. I must say that. Now about Richard…[Pause} Richard's character was definitely a person who ignorance became an impediment to his intellectual and social development. His ignorance was due to being dirt poor. Dirt poor in a major city means you are ill prepared to do anything meaningful. So, making a living is out of the question. Operating as though he still lives in the country means that this invisible native son is operating in a circle that is out of his element. His ill preparation is complemented with his inability to overcome his feeling of total inferiority to European Americans.

Tanesha

Yea, I know his kind. He would become totally subservient to a "white man" and kill a "nigger" at the drop of a hat.

Invisible Native Son

I dare you Nigger. I double dog dare you. If you just act like you gon' mess with me, I'll strike you dead rat there on the spot.

Tanesha

Stereo-type, nothing but a stereo-type. That character was not real, he was playing. The character was best acted by Steppin' Flechin.'

Nefatari

You know this is beginning of the nigger construct. Under this construct the Nigger is one who catered to white people, excuse me Miles and kill another African at the smile on his face. Now, this personality is definitely considered the Nigger personality. This is why black people, excuse me again Miles, are so offended when somebody European American calls one of them by the N...word. That's the origin of the Nigger construct. You see, the Nigger is a coward who will kill his brother if it means saving his own life. He would rat out on his once moon coon, his main man. However, when approached by the most favored, he to bows and scraps...

Invisible Native Son

Yassa miz Sally, yassa mr. Charlie, I'ze show will tak care dat Nigga for yo, jus leav' it to me. I'm mo' kill dat up-ti race Nigga for yo mr. charlie.

Miles

Hold up, Hold up. There are those who say that to the man, then curse his when his ass is out of sight. One person that happened to got word that mr. Charlie over heard him and got out of town, went into hiding underground because his life was thought to be at stake.

Tanesha

That may be so, but, it never happened to any one of the assassinated race people that we know about, did it? Like Fred Hampton, or Malcolm X or Medgar Evers.

SOCC

It never happened to anyone I know, if the man gave the word that he had to go. It never happened to the person I know.

Signify

So the powerlessness of the invisible native son created by Richard Wright made alienation a process of denial and non-recognition.

Miles

Hate to get deep, but you are advancing denial and non-recognition as the duality De Bois spoke of? Is that your point?

Ida B

Denial and non-recognition are twin constructs where one does not operate with out the other. Whether the case is powerlessness or helplessness, denial and non-recognition must be present for the alienated soul to feel a sense of defeat.

Nefatari

Alienation is a state of de-homeostasis, i.e., a state whereby the estranged personality cannot operate with the satisfaction of being well. The self feels a sense of nothingness, that is, of not being whole mentally: A distance between the physicality and the mentality serves to divide the body and personality into competing systems. The spiritual self feels lost, i.e., it is not present as of no value.

Ida B

So what you are saying is there is no sense of purpose, no reason for being, no desire for fulfillment, no longing for love,...

Tanesha

I might put it differently. I think I would say, a longing for love, a desire for fulfillment, a reason for living, a desire for freedom.

Miles

The point that we have avoided in this conversation is the role oppression plays in ones alienation. Oppression is the most important variable juxtaposed with freedom. It is the desire for freedom or jubilee than allowed the slave to submerge a great deal of the alienation that came along with social oppression legally enforced. With song and dance much of the pain of suffering was overridden by these activities of play. Play served to mitigate and sometimes negate the intended impact of the social oppression consciously imposed on those conquered and enslaved.

Nefatari

With Eurocentric opposition to song and dance as it revealed its spiritual components many slaves responded by "joining the church of" the master thereby attempting to gain some advantage in the process of adjusting to the rules of bondage. They cooperated with the oppressor in attempting to remove blues called Devil Songs from the confines of the slave quarters revealed how alienation can cause many to forego their old cultural forms simply to get relief from the terror suffered from the oppressor.

Miles

As in the case, Richard Wright's invisible native son's alienation caused him to expect the worse before it happened, thus causing it to happen. It is his equivocation as an omnipresent phenomenon that premeditates his tragedy.] He presupposes that the sky is going to fail, so he fails.

Signify

I see you maintain that he fails because fate has been decided already.

Miles

Not fate, position. His least favored position had been so internalized that he saw no successful way of negotiating a system he had no understanding of. He was at a total loss as to what to do. The matter was, all of this fear had been psychologically induced. Just the thought of what an officer of the law does to colored folks in Chicago put fear of horror in the invisible native son. There was no place to run, no place to hide, nowhere to go.

Tanesha

I liked what Richard Wright does, but, I get so angry with his character being so dumb. He cannot get anything right. He makes you too angry and wants to cry with his inability to do anything without messing it up. You just want to murder him. How can anybody be that dumb?

Nefatari

That is the question raised by everyone who sees the film or read the book. I am sorry to say this but the terror was so prevalent all over the country that no one of African ancestry felt safe.

SOCC

Terror, Terror was everywhere, it was over here, it was over there. Terror, terror was every where, every where. Alienation may be hard too bear, but terror, terror was every where, every where. Alienation may be hard to wear, but terror, terror is every where, every where.

Tanesha

How did they deal with it?

Miles

This was the ethos under which both writers wrote their novels. Things were bad. People traveling across the country going down south knew when to drive through the different parts of the country. And the drive was non-stop. Only gasoline was expected from the service station. People would drive all night from Los Angeles, California to Taylor, Texas.

Tanesha

The thing to understand is, despite all of the overt oppression, African intellectuals such as Duke Ellington, Ella Fitchgerald, Louis Armstrong, Marian Anderson, Zora Neale Hurston, Ralph Bunch, Ella Baker, Josephine Baker, Nella Lawson, Julian Percy, George Washington Carver and others advanced human understanding beyond the barriers erected by the culture of whiteness.

Signify

Did they suffer from alienation?

Miles

Of course! We all suffer from alienation. The degree we suffer is what makes it so strange we are suffering in the house we built. That is what makes it so devastating. This is home. You are not supposed to feel alienation at home.

Tanesha

That bring us to the topic of the music that has been identified with the word alienation from its coining: that is the blues.

Miles

Blues, simply blues. This music we call blues is not a vernacular, it may be considered folk, but it is not vulgar or primitive so to call it by a vernacular such as "the blues" is insulting and unnecessary.

Nefatari

I get your point immediately. Spiritual use to be called the spirituals and at some point the "the" was dropped and people simply called it spirituals. We should do the same for blues, is that your concern?

Miles

Blues is an art form. It is neither, secular or sacred. That is an invention of the culture of whiteness.

Tanesha

Culture of whiteness? Uh, huh! Now, what is the culture of whiteness? Is that like black popular culture?

Miles

Yes, it is.

Signify

So, haw did the culture of whiteness become responsible for making us call it the blues?

Miles

Oh, it started out very innocently.

SOCC

Like, "So what was that you play, Ray?

Ray (RSVP)

The blues, I was simply singing the blues.

Nefatari

Yes, but it became associated with a particular psychology?

Tanesha

And, that is?

Nefatari

Alienation.

Mind Boggled

WOW! AIN'T THAT NOTHING, WE SEGUA, RIGHT BACK INTO THE, PRIMARY TOPIC TODAY? THAT'S HEAVY [Pause] HOW THAT JUST HAPPENED.

Signify

How did it happen that blues became associated with alienation?

Miles

It was the delivery, how a lyric poet rendered the piece. People called it the blue because it was so slow, deliberate and carried so much pathos that it made it sound blue as in Miles Davis music. So the name is appropriate. There is nothing wrong with the name.

Tanesha

Now that you are forcing me to recall, I recall when the
Okays have all of these definitions of how name blues came about.

Signify

Like what?

Tanesha

Like Blue Devils they gave us drugs called red devils.

Nefatari

Do not go any further. As soon as the Europeans finally understood parts of the construct they decided that it came from their cultural forms.

Miles

The culture of whiteness.

Tanesha

That is obviously a lie. Europe had nothing to do with the origin of this music we call Blues.

Signify

That is a good way for me to ask this question, where did blues come form?

Miles

Phew! That is at least two volumes on Devil Songs. Well in my research over the past twenty years of reading the Born in Slavery slave narratives of 1936-37 I can say unequivocally blues has it beginning in Africa, Ethiopia, to be exact. We can trace it back to the Ethiopian scale that I suppose was popular in Solomon's Court and the empires of KMT pronounced KeMeT.

Nefatari

What we call Egypt today. GO ON MILES.

Miles

I have, also, discovered the music is in Congo, Mali, Ghana, Senagambia, St. Bartholomew, on an old Swedish Colony, in the Lesser Antilles of the Caribbean Small Islands. I have this piece called "A Melancholy Song without Drum" or something like that I discovered in an article in the Caribbean journal. What better way to tell the listener what genre the song is than by naming the song "A Melancholy Song Without Drums." This is a gift.

Signify

Okay, so how did it get the reputation of being a way of describing sadness, when somebody is down and out?

Miles

Oh, that is legitimate, but that is only one genre of the blues repertoire. And, I am not speaking about Jazz, RB, Gospel and Rock n' Roll. That is another story. I mean within the old form itself blues has always been used for other purposes.

Signify

Like what?

Miles

Like social or political commentary. Blues has always been the vehicle of commentary. Social, political, historical, you name it. Social may very well be a commentary on a particular act that was committed the day before or something like that. That is no less social commentary than the one that comes from a political statement in verse.

Tanesha

Okay, Miles I understand your point but what does all of that have to do with alienation?

Miles

One reason is the lyric poet who is responsible for its perpetuation has always lived a life of modesty to the point of being down right poor. Their habits often gave them the appearance of down and out. Some of these musicians were the hobos, the vagabonds, the gamblers, the abusers of alcohol, drugs and what ever else came along at the time while others went the other direction. But they were different they were intellectuals. They were excellent listeners, composers of the spoken word, readers of the times, change agents, and non-conformists. Often times, it is, they would be among the most alienated. Often they were the estranged par excellence if I may?

Nefatari

Estranged par excellence? Is that not an, what do they call it, oxymoron?

Miles

They were, [pause with example first just thought of it] look at Charlie Parker and Miles Davis.

Signify

I thought you were not talking about Jazz?

Miles

Oh, I am not.

Signify

Charlie Parker, Miles Davis are Jazz musicians, aren't they? I always thought they were?

Miles

Have you ever listened to Miles Davis? Have you ever heard Charlie Parker?

Signify

Yes,…

Miles

What did you hear?

Ida B

[Singing with Streams of Consciousness Choir SOCC] Many musicians do this by making sounds that translate into colors harmonically arranged to create streams of thoughts expressed musically. Improvisation of a composition at this level requires listening with great technical skill that comes from constant practice and experimentation with the scales, sound, texture, fluidity and other forms of musical distinction.

[Signify is trying to understand the question and Ida B hits him or I should say them with a brilliant song about the thing they should be listening for. Heavy shit!]

Tanesha

Oh, I understand. I just thought about Miles doing Kind of Blue, Porgy & Bess, and Sketches of Spain. They are the most beautifully blues tones I've ever heard. What makes it blues?

Miles

It is the tones that are created by applying what we call the minor scales. But I prefer to call them minor tones because there are more tone than are noted on the western piano. Don't get me wrong the tones are there. However, the Eurocentric construct of music disallows one to hear the others. As I discovered while watching the piano tuner tune the piano to the key of the Marimba family of instruments so that the piano would not be "off key". I offered I noticed this rather frequently, especially with the electric bass.

Signify

Hold up, I want you to go back to that minor tone construct, what was that? Oh I got the idea, thanks Tell the Truth. I never would have thought of that. My focus was too narrow. Now, Miles what is this minor tone idea you keep throwing out there?

Miles

The minor tones seem to be the notes that African, Indians, West Asians, and African Americans tend to generate their music and lyrics around. Listen to Lightin' Hopkins or Muddy Water or Santana or John Lee Hooker or Jimmy Reed or Bessie Smith, then roll out some Charlie Parker, Freddie Hubbard, Billy Holiday, Cassandra, Judy Bady, Diana Washington, John Coltrane, Eric Dolphy, [pause] the list is endless.

Signify

Just what should I be listening for?

Tanesha

Sound. Does it sound good to you and Why? Remember "why" is a subjective here. I may be wrong about this but aesthetics is probably one of the few philosophies that permit why as a question that may be asked, that can be asked as a search for what is pleasing. Why do I like that song? How on the other hand is difficult to ask as an aesthetic question. How does the song please me? Is kind of awkward....

Nefatari

Listening to your analysis, [Pause] "where" is it pleasing to me, is a rather awkward question to ask aesthetically speaking, also.

Signify

Yes, but what does that have to do with alienation?

Miles

Everything! Creative people are often better couriers of alienation than the people who actually feeling that way. And, in the case of the Be Bop musicians especially the ones who became ex-patriots when they moved to Europe were definitely alienated.

Nefatari

And then there's always Charlie Parker. He suffered an extreme sense of alienation. No one could express the music of alienation better than he could.

Tanesha

Now, Charlie Parker was the genius. His alienation did not hamper his ability to invent a whole new musical form that changed modern music.

Miles

As we see, alienation does not have to hamper creativity.

Tanesha

Well, we know that some claim that it is the alienation of the least favored that produces creativity or I might say advances the process. Check out Mozart. He and Yard bird were one of a kind. They set the standard.

Miles

That is so true. It is musicians like this who created whole new musical forms changed culture. We must remember that it was Be Bop that created a whole new vogue. Scat, jive talk, zoot suits, snappy dress,...

Tanesha

It also created a drug craze that wiped out a generation of musicians and other gofers.

Miles

That is true. So true! Alienation at it most extreme! This period was a true testament. Things were bad very bad then.

Nefatari

This brings us back to Ralph Ellison and Richard Wright.

Miles

That is true. Interesting how each was heavy into Jazz music.

Nefatari

Are you saying that the two novelists used letters to express what Charlie Parker, Dizzy Gillespie, Bud Powell, Max Roach, Charles Mingus, Thelonious Sphere Monk, the MJQ who set the standard that has never been compromised.

Signify

What do you mean Nefatari?

Miles

She means that after that if can not burn your ax you better get off the band stand.

SOCC

Alienation may be the estranged bedfellow, the sister follower of down trodden people who occupy the least favored position. But I can assure you that the creative spirit makes the alienated a gift to culture, a procurer of aesthetics, an inventor of artistic expression.

Reframe

So all we are here to do is tell the truth, tell the truth, tell the truth.

SOLO

Say it again, say it again, say it again. [Repeat]

Reframe

We are here to tell the truth, tell the truth. Tell the truth.

Signify

So will alienation ever be removed from the human soul?

Miles

I do not think so until there is a transformation to a society that practices an egalitarian system.

Nefatari

What is your point, Miles? What is the way to overcome alienation?

Miles

Wholeness!

Signify

Wholeness? What wholeness? What is wholeness?

Miles

Wholeness can only come when the tendency toward creating a society whereby self actualization is the norm rather than a fantasy that is super=ceded by the desire for material rewards.

Tell the Truth

Obviously your position is for alienation to go away we must create a society that promotes the notion that calls for "out of many one people" an old Jamaican motto we can all practice.

Miles

It would take making only a few changes in the polity of culture.

Ida B

What are you thinking of Miles?

Miles

If merit were the true norm in the civilian world of our civic society, alienation could be challenged into creative labor and other activity.

Nefatari

The problematic with that is the whole process of merit would have to be discovered another way from these bull shit tests everybody is suppose to rely on.

Miles

Oh, there are plenty ways that are available. I like the idea of the musician or something down in Land of Make Believe has put into practice.

Tanesha

Who is that, Miles?

Miles

I heard it on public radio. There is this person down in Venezuela, South America who take a quarter of a million of the least favored children and give them musical instruments and allow them to learn music.

Signify

For what purpose?

Nefatari

To let the crème rise to the top.

Miles

but he is doing something else.

Signify

What is that?

Miles

He is allowing the gifted to have instruments that will give them an opportunity to invent whatever musical idea your mind can uncover. With that many, all coming from the slums, it is impossible to determine the number of very gifted and potentially talented souls who may be discovered who otherwise may never be.

Nefatari

These are to dispossessed, the throw away I didn't want you babies.

Tanesha

The ones that are reported to be killed in Rio right on the street.

Ida B

I wonder what happens to the bodies.

Signify

What do you mean?

Ida B

Well isn't the stem cell research going on down there?

Invisible Native Son

Well, are you alleging that they are killing the dispossessed to use their body "parts,"

Tanesha

That is inclusive I take it.

Invisible Native Son

Well, in a society where you can kill the least favored and receive no punishment, human science is bound to have a win fall, a gold mine so to speak. Bodies unaccounted for may become the base of a whole new industry.

Ida B

That is true, I never developed it that far, but you are right.

Invisible Native Son

Would you call Brazil a product of the culture of whiteness, or should I call it western civilization?

Miles: Yes, I would think so.

Invisible Native Son

Is Brazil a state capitalist enterprise?

Ida B

Yes, it is.

Invisible Native Son

That seems like an ideal place to engage in all kinds of human sciences research, especially stem cell research.

Ida B

WOW! What a way to get the Ginny pigs to conduct the experiment.

Signify

Is that the decadents' way of making their contribution to science?

Miles

Yes they call them little Urchins. The only good that is realized is the murdered Urchins give their lives to science unwillingly and with malice as the intent of the kill.

Invisible Native Son

Do you think that receiving body parts in that manner should or at least ought to create negative energy that brings unpredicted nightmares or harm to the recipient.

Nefatari

You know, this conversation has taken an interesting turn right about now.

Invisible Native Son

Death at an early age was their fate. Then to exploit that dastardly deed, the killer or someone else will steal the half dead body and sell it to a human scientist so that he may have a chance to advance science. I had to join in because the murdered children might have been either one of us. We had it bad, but they had no chance. You see, "in humanity lay ones flaws as well as ones virtues." This comes from "Juneteenth" by Ralph Ellison.

Ida B

Society has reached an extremely low level of advancement when you may kill someone simply because that person is a have not.

Invisible Native Son

What makes the killing so senseless is it is carried out by a wanna be. [Pause] Someone attempting to improve there ranking.

Miles

You know, just thinking about it, alienation is not limited to the least favored people in a given society, it can permeate a whole nation, e.g. Burma. Alienation of the most favored who is "successful." is not addressed in a manner that permits us to study it.

Sta-tus Quoh

I have been sitting over here listening to your conversation and, I must say, it has been very interesting and stimulating. With that observation, all I have to say to you people is, you should be happy to be here. Look at the conversation you have been able to carry on without interruption, all we ask of you is not to make waves and try hard to fit in and we will get along just fine. Yawl, have a good day.[Sta-tus Quoh now stands up and leaves. Conversant are astounded, look in amazement as the intruder leaves.]

THE END

CRY OF MY PEOPLE
(On Birth Rights)

Act 1
Scene 1

POET SAID

>She sat silently
>Tears on her cheeks
>Sorrow in her eyes
>Joy long past
>A long time ago
>Overdue no more

>Eons of pain
>Sufferings of hardship
>Ending life

>Unending ……..

(Passing by is another speaker):

STREET MERCHANT
You wanna buy a stereo set, cheap? Hey, brother-man?

POET SAID
Unending,……..

(As a bystander):

CYNICA
Will it be this way all-the-time?

POET SAID

She sat silently
Tears in her eyes
Sorrow on her cheeks
Overdue joy
Long past
No more

Eons of pain
Suffering is hardship
Life ending
Unending…….

(Passerby speaks):

STREET BEGGAR

You gotta quarter you can spare, sister?

POET SAID

Unending now…….

(Bystander)

SCEPTICO

"Will my life be this way, all-the-time?"

(Citizen makes observation – lights Fade)

OLD LADY

Don't move so fast, that you don't know where you're goin.
(Voice of Streams choir singing) (Gospel style)

STREAMS

Freedom – we want freedom!
Freedom – give us our freedom!
Freedom – everybody wants freedom!

JABBO

I'm sorry, what did you say, just now? My mind was elsewhere. I only caught a glimpse of your – what you said. Everything happened too fast.

(Alluding to the poem, question & song)

OLD LADY

Don't move so fast that you don't see where you are headed, is what I said. You know people can get so caught up in what they are doin that they never find out what it is they (pause) do. The result is we go through life without ever realizing why.

JABBO

What prompted you to say that? It wasn't the poem we just heard. That was about a woman, a sad woman or maybe it was about women in general, the oppression of women in general. But how did you tie it into your statement about life?

OLD LADY

I hadn't thought about it until you raised the question, but now that I think about it, it sounded more like those parables Jesus Christ was so famous for. He told great stories, I'm told.

JABBO

What so you mean?

OLD LADY

You remember those stories Christ told to make his point: That was the poet.

THOUGHTFUL SOUL

Interesting! I clearly forgot about that. I was thinking about King Solomon's works of art that were contained in the Holy Scriptures. So, maybe we are thinking along the same lines. Solomon was a poet.

JABBO

Wait! Wait! I'm lost! I really don't know what you two are talking about.
You've lost me.

JABBO'S FRIEND

Yea, me too. Long time ago.

THOUGHTFUL SOUL

Well, in the Holy Scriptures, Solomon is credited with writing parts of Psalms, Proverbs, and Songs. In hearing Christians discuss "Songs of Solomon", as they are called, it is obvious that most think Solomon was writing about a people's struggle, a people's suffering, longing.

JABBO'S FRIENDS

What are the personal loses?

STREET MERCHANT

A first claim based on Birth Right.

JABBO

What was that?

JABBO'S FRIEND

Can you repeat that, again?

OLD LADY

Birth Right! People's Birth Right!

JABBO'S FRIEND

Excuse me, but what the hell is Birth Right? And, how does that relate to the poet's poem about the lady. (Still unconvinced by the conversation up to this point).

(Spoken by the narrator, while players are visual) (Players can be seen talking)

NARRATOR

However, you must admit that the points raised have been interesting, so far. The question is what are they getting at. They keep raising these points I've never thought of before. It's almost embarrassing; I can hardly keep up with the conversation. Am I that far out of touch with my current events? Really, it's not even current events, it's more like poetry, literature, law, religion, philosophy, politics. Things I've never…. Yes, Politics! That catchall phrase for an unexplained event. You know, like they were fired from their positions because it's "political". Anyway, where am I?

NARRATOR

Why am I doing this? I seem to be trying to gain some sense of what's going on. I don't seem to have a grasp of what is happening, is what's going on is really what's going on.

(Right back to players as though they were talking/nothing has interrupted the process they were engaged in.)

JABBO

And, can someone tell me what's going on? Seems like a time lapse, but I don't remember anything (Pause) happening. You know the feeling?

JABBO'S FRIENDS

I know exactly what you mean. I felt all of these thoughts. Really, I thought I was talking to you, but somehow it seemed unreal. I can't remember what it was. This conversation seems so unreal. Black people do not have these kinds of conversation. This is not us. We don't have..... (Demonstration outside the hall can now be heard in full BLAST!)

REPORTER

The demonstrators are very awkward at this point because the demonstration was called at a moment's notice. The opposition? Prof. Torts, a very noted barrister in Great Britain before he became interested in the "Philosophy of Artificial Intelligence", has been invited to give a lecture at City Institute for the Study of Intellectual Development (CIF – SID!) on his new theory of intellectual development. "Yearning" Theory, as he calls it. Excuse me, viewers and listeners, one of the organizers of the demonstration is about to speak. Let's see who that is? Yes, it's Abdul Haqmed in the Kill Racist Coalition, pronounced KRACK, is about to take the podium. Abdul Haqmed!

(Dramatized like rally in African American community in1986) (Muslim greeting)

ABDUL HAQMED

Brothers and sisters and comrades I'd like to take the opportunity to thank yawl for coming out to protest this racist action today.   As you know, today is the day of Respect! Everybody rise! Lower your heads!

(20 Seconds with "In a Silent Way" by Miles Davis Playing in the background)

Thank you! Thank you comrades, brothers and sisters. Why are we here today, I'm sure many of you are asking. Well, we just got word last night that Prof. Torts was invited to speak at the Important Hall, City Institute for the Study of Intellectual Development (CIF –SID).Who is Prof. Torts? Prof. Torts is ....(Interruption from Rally Participant.)

RALLY PARTICIPANTS

...... Hey man, cut the bullshit and let's get on with the show. I ain't here to hear no speech about no racist we already know.

(Streams enter as a "Greek" chorus – back up)

STREAMERS

Hey man cut the bull and let's get on with the show. I ain'there to hear no speech about no racist we already know.

(Rapid: One at a time)

What do you know? What do you know? What do you know?
(Haqmed catches on fast, makes necessary adjustment.)
Addresses Crowd –

HAQMED

I know we going to go into that lecture hall tonight and establish once and for all who has the right to the original position on this hemisphere, who has first right claim to the new world musical expression of New World culture. Ain't that right?

(Feeling good about his conquest)

RALLY PARTICIPANTS

Right on, brother man! Say it again! Everybody didn't hear you!

(Confidence and enthusiasm) (Louder)

HAQMED

I said that we are going inside CIF –SID and determine who's boss. Is it we? Or, is it they?

(Satirical):

ALL STREAMERS

Is it we? Or, is they? Is it us? Or, is it them?

(Frustrated with the playful nature of the streams.)

RALLY PARTICIPANTS DON'T PLAY

Fuck that! That ain't no argument. "They or them", we know who he's talking about.

(FRUIT OF ISLAM move in to take 'DON'T PLAY' away from the crowd. Don't want any "agents" stirring up the crowd.)

STREAMERS

(Again, showing satire) (No condescension) Is it we? Or, is it they? Is it us? Or, is it them?

RALLY PARTICIPANT DON'T PLAY

Who is he talking about? Man, who are these dudes? Where they come from? They friends of yours? If they don't shut up, I'm going to kick me some ass. This is serious business, We ain't got time for jiving around. Excuse me, Bullshit! You better take them dudes out-a here befo' I loose my kool.

STREAMERS

Chill out! Chill out!

(F.O. I. move to either side of DON'T PLAY just as he was about to move toward the STREAMS. Before surprise takes him, he is wisped out of the picture. Audience applaud.)

WHITE ACTIVIST SUPPORTER:

Yea, let's get on with the show.

(Demonstrators head into Important Hall to hear lecture. As demonstrators arrive, the lecture has not begun so they assume the stage to let their poet laureate "set the tone" for the evening's lecture.)

(Music heard behind the poet is a Randy Weston composition)

(Low reporters voice) (Again with Mike in hand)

REPORTER

The demonstrators have arrived before the lecture and have taken the initiative to allow one of their noted poets, Poet Said Saud read some of his "poetry" This is an uninvited reading I must inform you viewers and listeners. But, apparently a discussion has been held and, an agreement has been reached (Show parties arguing, then agreeing) between KRC pronounced KRACK, and the sponsors of the lecture, CIF – SID, the City Institute for the Study of Intellectual Development. Poet Said Saud is now heading toward the podium again. As you recall, he had been placed there only to be removed, and now he's back again. Let's see what Poet Saud has to say.Listening viewers, Poet Said Saud.

(Muslim greeting! Then Filler Buster)

POET SAID:

I'd like to thank you brothers and sisters and comrades for letting me come before you tonight. With such short notice, I thought I'd share with you one of my "Jazz" poems written for our immortal Randy Weston. I wrote this poem while sitting at the New Muse in Brooklyn, N.Y. Randy was giving a free concert for us bloods who can't afford to hear our music anymore. Yawls know what I mean. Right brothers and sisters!

(Audience response is positive) RIGHT ON!! (Pause – tone is set) (Slap five)

(Total Silence)

POET SAID:

What are they trying to tell us? I wondered, is it that we have no need to feel apart from each other? The drum hummed while a piano rang sounds of the African musical equation, our version, of course. The new was old was new again. His idea was to communicate in a language about a force greater than our will to be.

(Randy Weston with Addison Weston on congas and Talib Kibwe on alto sax playing.)

The past was present! The future was here. A new voice was heard between the keys/impressions of a rhythm so often denied its place in the sun. It is, our sun I am referring. The one that contains the essence of our collective lives. Our united being. So? Where will we go next as we search around, in between, all about our own equation/definition of reality? What is our purpose for being?

(New thought enters) (Weston still playing)

POET SAID

The music played - he played for us - was the answer to our riddle: Is it possible to move at our speed with no history, and so much opposition? But, like a lost people, we are unable to see the Messenger, our prophet, when he performs right before us.

(Now, right to the question) (Weston still Playing!)

What are the problems of a people who are forever lost in their search for themselves? (Pause) To assure us that WE ARE ONE - that we are the ONES that – He came to communicate with, i.e., to talk to, if you will, to let us know that the sound was authentically REAL: There is a reality we can claim. There are rights to our birth! We can claim an original position, in the future new world.

(Description of Randy's Movement) – (Strong Weston now)

The Composer – our Messenger – moves forward as he goes back into our time, our space – you see, everybody has a space in this universe, on this earth – He combines our roots with each other: soldiering them, those severed roots buried in a foreign soil of human suffering, anger, pain, oppression, love ….. (Pause)

How can sound waves that are so near/How can voice sounds that are so dear – become so unreal to us? (Dramatic) to our ears? (Pause when they are played back to us.) (Short pause) In time? By those among us who have bothered to search out our history where a search must be carried out? Where? Where? (Louder) (Answer) At home, of course!

Is it, we are afraid to know – to give – because to know – to give means we must know something about our suffering?

Is it, we really are not aware that mathematics and music evolved out of the same equation? Are related in time and space? As time and space?

Didn't we learn that the drum is universal – multi-versal in time and space? That it travels along the same electrometric waves as all other equations? That the drums taught us time? How to count? That our definitions of time/space can be heard through the rhythms of before? That the relativeness of things and properties is such that they are often expressed in the exactness of our multi-theme foundation?

POET SAID

(Speaking as a storyteller) A music (Pause) A people's music is an expression of their being; where they are — How they are doing. A music that becomes mechanical reveals its separate-ness of from people. It shows a failure to appreciate what we all must know as we search—(Pause) a failure to appreciate what we all must know-- as we search out our destiny.

(Revelation) (Pause) But others know. They know the value of our music, so often, long before we have come to recognize its beauty. (Moderator gets anxious) (Audience is attentive)

So! They sit among us and listen, to hear, see, and eventually claim its value for themselves while we venture into new unexplored territories, evolving our creative labor, unaware of the connection between what we are trying to create and the necessary unity of a people's history.

So, as I said, others sit unannounced, unpretentiously listening, learning, trying to acquire the essence of what we take for granted…… (As though moving on) (Back to music) ….. The limitation of His instrument of creative labor and expression were under-stood, but he continues to push, press, out of frustration, out of a desire to make us hear, aware of how it all means one thing.

(A tone of frustration –but observation)

Somehow the instrument he played would not suffice, so he added a son with a drum – a more fluid instrument of creative labor: One more in tune with our verse – an instrument not of artificial creation – more organic – social – (Now referring to father and son) (Summary) And, they played together, as one. Then – the music began to flow forth as if – out of nowhere – No! - Everywhere …..

(Finished, applause, exit stage)

(The speaker for the evening, Prof. Torts, understands the dynamic that has gone down, so without introduction, he approaches the stage and podium. He moved "down front" when the demonstrators entered to get a better "seat" to see the action)

{Reporter enters, speaks quietly to the listening audience.}

REPORTER
……….. Listening viewers, apparently the guest lecturer, Prof. Torts, feels he needs no introduction because he has approached the podium unannounced. Let's hear what he has to say. (Fades out)

PROF. TORTS
I say poof, poof, to you!

(The unexpected statement cause unexpected reactions)

(And, he continues) (Audience laughs, then realizes he's the opposition. Immediate silence follows.) As a Barrister for the Queen, I found the demonstration very well staged. My "Hats off to you."(In a Cambridge accent) Let me say further, that I'd be a fool to try and compete with you. On the contrary, I shant fight with you at all.

I am here to engage in serious dialogue, as)(just before someone in audience was about to respond.) I see that you (Pause, looks right at the audience) are. However, (humorous) I must admit you caught me completely (embarrassing the moderator) by surprise, as I'm sure you did to our distinguished moderator.

(Audience laughs as moderator turns as red as a beet.) But I'm not a sore loser, and I love surprises that are well staged. Even if the aim is to disrupt my lecture. You see, it gives me more press. The more controversial I am especially if I did not orchestrate it – the more readers hear about me, the more books I sell. So, you see, you never know where a gift may come from.

(Laughter) (Not impressed)

PROF. TORTS
Okay, now for my lecture for the evening. I'd like to begin by thanking the City Institute for inviting me to your great institution, and allowing me to enter a format that will expose some of the ideas I've been pondering for the last twenty years. I welcome dialogue! Now, on with the lecture, (Pause) with your kind permission, of course. If I can pick up from where the demonstrators began, I think the point is, learning is a multifaceted process that encompasses the ability to understand – comprehend – as a dialectical outgrowth of discovery, imagination, and observation: Learning combines the intellectual capacity to "think" with other senses operating within the physical realm of our existence, i.e., the human brain uses our ability to "think" to verify sub/objective reality in terms of our own existence, as reported by our senses.

In other words, in terms of the human equation – to use one of your terms – learning is an intellectual process that combines the energies of the brain – inclusive of the nervous system – in such a way that one is able to make some sense out of the "real" world. (Prof. Torts picks up speed in his delivery here) So the world is as we perceive it to be, and it is not! It is what we learn that it is, and it is not. It is more, different, better, worse, etc., etc., depending on where you are in time and space your relative perspective on life reflects your relative position in life. (More speed)

At first, I suspect, what we discover in life may happen at random, then maybe by trail and error, and eventually, hopefully by more consistent forms and means of reason and logic, i.e., more consistent forms and means of reason and logic, i.e., more consistent way of understanding "reality".(Hold!)

The goal of learning – if I may become subjective for a moment and I say learning has a "goal" or a reason for taking place if learning has a goal, it is to understand, not knowledge for its own sake, or in its own abstraction, but to understand the nature (culture) of one's own reality, and how that reality connects with the rest of the universe.

(By now, part of the audience is intently listening while the other part is "bored".) (Faster.)

The basis of learning is – if I may now become an objective scientist – the simultaneity of thought and activity, i.e. we move about and we think. We think about out (Movement) activity and if we are conscious, we act on our thinking: Thought as an activity operates at the some time as the activity that stimulates thought – and I might add, all of the activity that goes on regardless of thought, out thought, that is. I don't want to show disrespect to those who believe in a supreme.

(Very fast delivery)

To continue, the effect of this simultaneity is to combine thought with the "material world", and to give reason to itself. Language allows us to explain thought and activity in the form of subject and object, person and other, being and becoming, as separate activities, separate processes.

Thus, we are able to consciously divide reality into many constituent parts by thinking of "it" that way. Our language is based on sound and speech, tomorrow's language will be based on the intellectual capacity of our artificial intelligence, the "computer". You see, to speak to a computer does not require sound or speech. So the language can and will evolve differently. (Pause)

(Now, slow delivery again)

PROF. TORTS

But right now, language allows us to communicate how we reflect upon our thoughts of the material world in terms of what that world means to us.

This is how – I suppose! - our expressions become the basis of our "culture." Our expressions become our culture, our culture, our expressions. Our language and cultural expressions become our lives of distinction.

(At this point, the "bored" group can take it no longer. As a matter of fact, this action is considered long overdue.)

Our lives become positioned according to the value we attribute to our collective language and culture. Our culture.....

(Now, the audience speaks.) (Unison)

ONE SIDE

A language for you and a language for me, first class citizens we shall be.

A language for you, and a language for me, first class citizens we shall be.

(In unison, the other side of the audience is up.)

OTHER SIDE

We are not passive absorbents who sit idly by while our sponges are poured into. No! We are human beings. Intellectual beings! You can't stand there and act as though there are no atrocities committed under the name of discovery, observation, and culture: As you say, that is your constituted right.

AUDIENCE

Lied about!

PROF. TORTS:

Oh! I beg to differ, we do not consider it lying so much as we believed it to be true. Obviously the white man's Egypt looks nothing like….

AUDIENCE

………….. That's mythology!

PROF. TORTS

Sure it is, but when the shoe is on the other foot it looks differently.

SMART ASS

Of course, no two worlds are the same; no two world views are the same, isn't that your point?

PROF. TORTS

Exactly! No two worlds, no two world views are the same. That is exactly my point. What are we to expect?

AUDIENCE

What do you mean?

SMART ASS

Yes, I'd like to hear that too, what do you mean, western scholars during the height of European invasion of Africa, Asia, and the Americas……?

BLOOD

………….. Don't forget Australia.

SMART ASS

…………. Right, Australians were no more knowledgeable of the world out side of their limited framework than were the peoples whose land they stole, is that your point?

AUDIENCE

Right! They simply had more firepower.

SMART ASS

Exactly, and a more efficient way of communicating.
We say, we shall not absorb!

(Streams begins to chant.)

STREAMS

Be it for REAL or on a screen, we shall not absorb.
Be it for REAL or on a screen, we shall n ot absorb.
Be it for REAL ………… (Fade out as Prof Torts speaks in response to the audience outcry.)

[Observing movement of Streams]
BYSTANDER

There they go back and forth. There they go back and forth.

{…Torts continues as though nothing has happened, but responding to the notion "we shall not absorb"]

PROF. TORTS

That may not be such a bad idea: That is, to sit and absorb, for a change. Then maybe we can get you hot-heads to think rationally for a change. We understand that frustration may act as a catalyst for aggressive creativity, but it may also lead to self-defeat. You know, where you are consumed by your own energy: The energy of your own creation; spontaneous internal combustion. The Human Torch! Like the Phoenix?

SMART ASS

Like Richard Pryor!

(Explaining why Richard Pryor was chosen.)

That's more real, less metaphorical, to me. It's less steeped in the mythology debate. Also, that example fits into the category of verifiable events western science finds so necessary.

AUDIENCE

You will admit that western social scientists have had difficulty relating Egypt to Africa though, wont you? And, to the African-American? Isn't the Phoenix Pryor connection contrary to the Africa western historians have constructed?

SMART ASS

Your mean, painted!

AUDIENCE

Lied about!

PROF. TORTS

Oh! I beg to differ, we do not consider it lying so much as we believed it to be true. Obviously the white man's Egypt looks nothing like.....

AUDIENCE

.... That's mythology!

PROF. TORTS

Sure it is, but when the shoe is on the other foot it looks differently.

SMART ASS

Of course, no two world's are the same; no two world views are the same, isn't that your point?

PROF. TORTS

Exactly! No two worlds, no two world views are the same. That is exactly my point. What are we to expect?

AUDIENCE

What do you mean?

SMART ASS

Yes, I'd like to hear that too, what do you mean, western scholars during the height of European invasion of Africa, Asia, and the Americas......?

BLOOD

.... Don't forget Australia.

SMART ASS

...... Right, Australians were no more knowledgeable of the world out side of their limited framework than were the peoples whose land they stole, is that your point?

AUDIENCE

Right! They simply had more firepower.

SMART ASS

Exactly, and a more efficient way of communicating.

AUDIENCE

Prof. Torts, would you say this was the beginning of artificial intelligence?

PROF. TORTS

Do you mean the printing press or the calculating machine?

BLOOD

Now that you mentioned them, obviously both.   I hadn't thought of it that way. "Them that way", sorry.

PROF. TORTS

Sure, automatic technology definitely may count that as its beginning; those two machines, if they continues development that began around the 15/16 centuries is your starting point.

(Now alluding to protest.)

Interesting that your frame of reference is so recent, being that you raised the question about the Phoenix and Africa's Egypt, I would have expected you to go much further back. However, I get your point.

(Taking the opportunity to address the Phoenix)

BLOOD

That's not quite how it happened, I mean, about the "spontaneous internal combustion" discussion we touched up on briefly. That's not how our birth rights were taken away.

(The audience is now shown two simultaneous versions of how "it" happened, one the colonized people's version, the other, the white man's version. This is done through total simultaneous imagery (TSI).)

PROF. TORTS

Or, signed away by treaty! Again, depending on whose version you accept as representing a more accurate picture of what happened.

(Note: Blood changes his language as he gets more comfortable.)

BLOOD

The thang is yawl always trying to get us to be "objective", or, willing to accept your version of what happened, ours simply gets lost in the process. We are simply lying?

PROF. TORTS

Why do you say that?

BLOOD
Because you write the books!

PROF. TORTS
If you mean we keep records, yes we do that, but that's so everyone will know what happened.

SMART ASS
We keep records, too. At least, we used to.

PROF. TORTS
Yes, but yours were not accurate.

SMART ASS
Why? Because we chose to keep our records orally? Is that suppose to be our fault? Our reason for being alienated from our Birth Rights? Is that our fault? Because you came and successfully uprooted us from our space, is that supposed to be our fault?

PROF. TORTS
The record is clear, you sold your land to the European settlers.

CARETAKER
How could we sell what was not ours to sell?

PROF. TORTS
That's not my problem, your ancestors knew what they were doing.

(Again, total simultaneous imagery (TSI): One depicting a native council agreeing to share common property in common with the European; the other depicting "a legal bill of sale transferring land from the "Indians" to the European settlers.")

SMART ASS
We suffer because you used words that had no meanings for. We suffer because what you provide us with has no meaning to us: That is the nature of our alienation under your rule.

(At this point a quit unassuming "Indian" speaks. Southwestern accent.)

CARETAKER
Exactly! We are permanently outlawed from what belongs to nature. We are nature's children. Take nature's children away from HER safekeeping, and nature will tremble this Earth in pain until those children are retuned to her. That is the word given to us by our ancestors. Our ancestors said that it was impossible for them to "give" or "sell" the Europeans any "property". They had no right by our spiritual custom to make such as sale or, "treaty", as Europeans call it.

It was not theirs to do, and they did not do it. We believe our ancestors. Therefore, nature's land was taken away from her caretakers. And, each generation that goes by without returning nature's land back to us, there will be greater and greater hardship as more and more of her earth is eaten away by the greed of western science and technology: MARK MY WORD!

CARETAKER
(Now he changes, emotion is shown.)

.....................And what so we have to show for it? High death rates, no work, no money, no land to cultivate. We have the dubious distinction of being the most exploited and maltreated of all "minorities" in the United States: That includes the African-American, the most widely discussed "minority" in this great land of ours, and the Mexican-American our blood brothers and sisters.

(Now with great pride.)

We are nations within a nation. Nations within nations if we include Mexico and Canada and Central America, on down below. Yet we – us, the native people of the Americas – find it virtually impossible to receive justice in "the most Democratic of Republics."

We have tried to live apart from these nations that consume us, but how?

(By now, everyone is listening with great intent.)

My question to you sir, you are a great scholar of your people. Tell me, are we suppose to be the model prototype of your new world arrangement? Are we the "Braves" in your Brave New World? Is how you treat us your representative ideal of tomorrow?

(With everyone focused on Caretaker's strong statement, the streams appear as the African Support Choir.) (Done as a "pop" tune/late 50's R&B.)

STREAMS
Is this for real? Are you always so ready to kill? Kill? Kill? Even the land that you steal? Is this for real?

(Fade out) (Repeat) (Prof. Torts loses his cool for a moment – recovers quickly.)

PROF. TORTS
I don't find these interruptions contributing to our discussion. As a matter of fact, I find them rather annoying.

(Streams appear, again   (To audience)

STREAMS
Is he for real? Does he not follow our appeal? (then looking at Prof. Torts) Are you for real? Is that the deal? Are you for real?

(Fade out)

(Prof. Torts now trying to conceal his anger with reason)

PROF. TORTS
You see, all these outbursts do are cause confusion, you don't want the truth to be heard.

(Audience)

(Serious challenge by Torts – Audience responds in kind)

AUDIENCE
Is he for real? HA! HA! HA! HA!

(Sort of embarrassed, perturbed with Torts)

WHITE ACTIVIST {This is a position not color of one's skin}

Sir, are you listening to what they are telling you? Can you hear? I think their questions are clear? At least, to my ear. (Laughter)

Should I repeat them for you? I happened to write them down just in case doing the course of the dialogue you might forget.

(Streams appear in sound – to be heard not seen)

(Question is very serious)

STREAMS

Is there no shame:

You are to blame! (Firm with authority-- not loud)

(Torts responds in kind. He believes what he's saying)

PROF. TORTS

I have no blame.

I have no shame.

Equity is my claim.

No Blame! No shame!

I have no reason to be ashamed. We live in the greatest civilization of all

times.   Look at our accomplishments in roughly two or three hundred years.

No other nat............

(Steams cut in.) (In National Anthem form)

STREAMS

...........nation that kills with pride, all of those who lived inside, will freedom ring?

Will freedom ring?

Will freedom ring?

(Audience gives a response to streams.)

AUDIENCE RESPONSE

Freedom – we want out freedom.
Freedom – give us our freedom.
Freedom – everybody wants freedom.

BLOOD

Sure, tell us anything homeboi. We know! The niggas – excuse us – injuns brought this on themselves. Sure, brother man, we know! HA! HA! Tell us anything, we don't know no better. HA! HA! HA! HA!

(Audience laughs, too)

(People are laughing while shaking their heads in disbelief knowing exactly what Prof. Torts meant.)

(Laughter stops simultaneously. One straggler shows mood with his bold laughter.)

PROF. TORTS

Mr. Moderator, I've had enough of these insults. Please control your audience or I shall have no choice but to conclude that I can no longer add any useful ideas to this discussion. I might add, such disruptions are a violation of my constitutional rights to free speech, and everybody else's right to assemble here freely, unmolested.

(Caretaker speaks in total disbelief. Raises question.)

CARETAKER

Do my people have a right to assemble freely on the land of our ancestors? Can we speak freely about how our birth rights were stolen from us? Huh? Can we do that without being called communists? What about our rights as self-contained nations?

PROF. TORTS

(To Caretaker)

What is your point? Mr. Moderator I've about had it up to here. (To Moderator with the emotional interruptions) I know that you people (To audience are caretaker).

AUDIENCE

You people? You people?

(The way Black people say it.)

PROF. TORTS

Yes, you people have had a rough go at it. But, that's not my fault, and I refuse to assume total responsibility for what might have happened to you in the past. That's all in the past, the unspeakable past. We must learn to let bygones be bygones. You must learn to live in the future.

(Watch here! Slow build up to argument)

AUDIENCE

The future is now! The past is upon us.

(Ignoring comment from audience.)

PROF. TORTS

Now, much of what you say is opinion.

AUDIENCE

Opinion? Our alienation, simply an opinion?

PROF. TORTS

No! No! Your observations.

AUDIENCE
Our deprivation?

PROF. TORTS
No, there is no duplication!

AUDIENCE
And, degradation?

PROF. TORTS
There's no verification of that.

AUDIENCE
You won't deny our subjugation!

PROF. TORTS
No, that's alienation!

AUDIENCE
Is that your observation?

PROF. TORT
You mean, your deprivation?

AUDIENCE
I mean you subjugation! (of us)

PROF. TORTS
There's no verification of your subjugation; no observation of any discrimination, no denial of your being, although your character may be questioned.

We are the future. There is no denial here. No distinctions are made here. We are one. There are no distinctions, here!

(Poet moves toward center stage repeating)

STREAMS
There are no distinctions; HERE!
Can't you see?
There's us and we!
And, we are free – or, (Pause)
is there a fee?

(Leave stage; streams – poet speaks as a continuation to the thought)

POET SAID
No thoughts, anyway.
So, why do I tremble?
Search? Wonder? Stumble?
Why can't I hear no dreams, anymore.

So, whom do I trouble?
Frighten? Threaten?
Whom do I threaten?

(Change)

(Response)

I think we have begun to listen! I think we have begun to hear!

(Questioning) Did you detect a slight contradiction, there? Yes, I would agree, but that is the nature of things here and now. Our new Politics of Culture.

We are ready to accept your observations Prof. Torts. No distinctions! Right now! Good! The Presidency! That's our first request!

(Looking of Prof. Torts saying, "I did not intend for it to be interpreted that way.")

(Poet rises again)

POET SAID

So whom do I trouble? Why do I tremble? Where do I wonder? Toward Pluto this time? Into a troubled world with a love of peace?

Will it be in this world? Or, the next? Our Love of Peace? And where are my dreams, anymore? Apparently, things are very satisfying, more and more! We live much better, now.

(Streams come and whisper to poet:)

They have invaded ANGOLA!

They have invaded GRENADA!

(Cry) Nicaragua, Mozambique, Wounded knee, Panama, Haiti, Dominican Republic, Somalia and Bosnia.

(As though nothing was whispered.)

(Feeling proud)

POET SAID

I live much better, now that there are no distinctions.

(With astonishment)

But, why are they crying? (Change – serious)

Tell me, why are there acts of rebellion in Central America so often? Why, all-the-time? And in Africa, too? Obviously, the counterbalance to our American Democracy is the oppression of her other Americas. The other Americas.

Oh! I know! You're living yours! Your heaven is not located in the beyond, in the hereafter! No! Your heaven is right here on earth. It's right, here. SEE! SEE! (With deep anger) SEE!

(Wonder) We kill a thirty-six year old Grenadian simply because he was so kind as to (Crying – can't finish) ……… as to (Really trying to comprehend.) How do we blow up a scholar like Walter Rodney? Please, explain? I don't understand! You say he was a communist?

Then, what about J. A. Rogers? We wouldn't publish his books. Why? And what happened to Albert Ayler? HA! HA! And, who is Albert Ayler? Huh? I bet you don't even know. I ought to embarrass, you (Looking right into the audiences' faces as one). Yea, that's right. I'd embarrass you over someone you ought to know.

Why should I allow you to allow our greatest creative gifts to remain anonymous, to us? HUH? NAW! NAW! (In street language) It ain't gone bees likes that!

I know you ain't never heard of Albert Ayler! I know! I know!

You don't know the names of who – let's see, who! - Let's say for the sake of argument – you don't know the names of three artists who died last year?

(With quick delivery)

Or, any of those people who were gunned down in your own community at the hands of a policeman's gun. Am I lying? I said, as I lying? I'm talking about ordinary people now.

(Baptist preacher, now)

You just name me one blood who you remember! Just one! One artist! One musician! Who made it past age 45.

(Back to poem)

No tear, all dry.

So, who keeps returning to the well?

Wishing? Crying? Confused?

(Now assuming the character of citizen)

Please Lord, let our leaders be telling the truth.

There must be meaning to our lives, Lord. Our adventures across the seas must be for peace, ARE THEY NOT, Lord. (Pause)

POET SAID

One simple question, why would our government destroy the New Jewel Movement papers? Excuse me, the Black Panther papers? And, what do you suppose happened to Adam's records? Who is Adam? Adam Clayton Powell! I know, there are so many, aren't there. But, Adam? You mean we can go almost anywhere we please now, and we don't even remember Adam? Phew! Now, that's heavy!

Anyway, let's go on. (Matter of factly) I've got you here so I might as well say what's on my mind. These occasion don't come that often. But the time has come, and if nobody but these walls hear what I speak, somebody's got to say it.

(Half humorously/half seriously)

Hell, I aint tryin to be no sacrificial lamb! I don't taste like lamb, anyway. That I am certain of. You may run with that as you please. But, we can't let the legend of Adam & A. Phillip & Dubois & Robeson & Mary McCleod & Fannie Lou & Rosa Parks & our slain die, too. We can't do that! That's suicide! Did you hear me folks. I said that is genocide! Fratricide! Do you get my point! (Then lightens up!)

You know where I'm coming from! It's only natural that now's the time. Now is the time, there's no serious debate about that! WE MUST MOVE! AS ONE!

AS ONE HUMANITY!

We have earned the right to PARTAKE IN, ALL offerings. All offerings. All of them! That includes the discussion around who has the right to declare us extinguishable. It's just that simple. It's just! That simple!

There is going to be an EARTH with people on it. People who look like you and me and us. The laws of distributive justice say that the social and the earth body must share equivalently, not in adverse proportions to individual and social wealth. WE WANT THIS EARTH KEPT ALIVE!

(The moderator approaches the podium for the first time, and interestingly, he appears confident.)

(Because what he is about to ask is so complex, yet so simple, it must be read or recited in a manner that allows everyone to – "get it" the first time. Now, it will be for a moment; and may people will ponder it further, that's O.K. It's difficult but let them feel the question. Feel it in essence.) (Listening)

MODERATOR

Mr. Speaker, Mr. Spencer-Brown, I believe a fellow countryman of yours has written in Laws of Form that "there can be no motive unless contents are seen to differ in value."

I suspect I lost most of you so I'll repeat again, Spencer-Brown said that "there can be no distinction without motive; and there can be no motive unless contents are seen to differ in value." You said, there are no distinctions, here. And, I take it you were limiting your comment to this room. So my question is, how would you define Birth Right as a first principle of culture.

PROF. TORTS

(Obviously, Prof. Torts was an excellent Barrister in Great Britain because, although the Moderator's question literally floored him, he recovered rather well.)

I'll be very honest, I was not prepared for today.
(Laughter)

But, let me try anyway. (Attention) I've never been so happy to have had legal training.

(Laughter. Referring to his background before becoming a "Philosopher of Artificial Intelligence" and how helpful it has been today, he goes right into......)

PROF. TORTS

What is rightfully yours at birth continues with you throughout life, unless that right is released to some else. (Hiss! Hiss! Hiss! Come from audience) For example, if you have the talent........ (He should always be heard clearly, not matter what) Let's say you have the ability to compose music lyrics and the score, I believe they call it. That's your talent, yours skill. And let's say that you wrote a beautiful ballad that you were sure would become a hit. However, there's a problem. No one will offer you a contract. Let's say further that you are accomplished as a musician. Here's the deal! A recording company representative stopped by the local

Five Spot and heard your group perform. He offered you a deal right there on the spot: The deal was how would you like to record for International Jazz? They – meaning International Jazz – would produce, etc, your album. You would record your music, with your group or with your selection of musicians. Whatever!

(Actor-Jazz musician appears)

JAZZ MAN

Oh, shit! Is this for real? Did you hear that, I-we-got a recording contract. We can make our record. Record our own music.

PROF. TORTS

You make your record. Record you music.small hit. In other words, you make it big as a jazz musician.

While listening to the radio one day someone very famous hears you LP and likes a particular tune: The Ballad! He calls up his manager, etc., etc.,

(Stop! Better Example)

They get your name, call you up and say….. No, let's make the even more direct. You are sitting, listening to the radio one day and your tune - The Ballad! - comes on sung by the famous pop star. You say, ………

JAZZ MAN

…..Oh! Shit! That's my song: That's my music "pop star" is singing there. Oh, shit! I'm going to be rich! And, famous, too.

PROF. TORTS

What you did not know was when you signed that recording contract, the only thing you were allowed to do was record your music. You didn't own the rights to "nothing". Not even your own music, recorded by you. Nothing!

Oh sure you become famous. People see you and say, "you're the one who wrote that beautiful ballad. Give me your autograph." Can you tell them, Jazz man?

JAZZ MAN

Yes, I wrote it, but it ain't mine! I don't own it. I released my rights to that tune when I cut my first album. Ain't that some shit!

NARRATOR

(The audience was stunned, This argument presented so well by Prof. Torts and verified by his witness to the facts, and all. As I said, Prof. Torts recovered from the question rather well. So the audience sat telling each other stories of a dude who don't get no royalties, and that 's his tune. He wrote it! His name is on it, but he can't collect a dime.)

(Then out of frustration.)

AUDIENCE

Prof. Torts what you say we know all too well, but that ain't the half of it. I can tell you……….

(Blood to the rescue.)

(Mingus composition plays as intro and throughout.)

AFRICAN CHOIR--WITH BLOOD
…… Mingus was Dead! Mingus was dead! Mingus was dead long before we recognized his genius.

BLOOD
Charles Mingus had to die before we knew that he had even lived. Such strange words from a people who created Mingus. Such irony of being!

CHOIR
(Sing) Such is the nature of becoming. Such is the nature of recognition.

BLOOD
Such a strange way for a people who have suffered so greatly, so long……

CHOIR
(Sing) Such is the nature of restriction/oppression.   Such is the nature of non-recognition, to never know, to overlook such a creative genius. Mingus the Genius. Mingus the Genius. The Genius of Mingus. Mingus the Genius. Mingus the Genius. The Genius of Mingus.

BLOOD
But, we never recognized his genius, his creativity while he lived. It's like we are determined to follow the dictates of others in spite of our intuitive inclination.

SMART ASS
Is this the proper way we should act? Playing the roles others have drawn out for us?

CHOIR
Yet, no respect is forth coming.

BLOOD
Still we do not know how much our ancestors gave to humanity.
(Becomes a Mingus Hymn, here)

CHOIR
Mingus had to die before we discovered he had ever been her with us. The Pathos of Americanism has caused us to disbelieve the value of our being. So Mingus/Hughes died and we sill do not know who they are. Their creativity unsurpassed and but we are told it's Styron/Faulkner whom we should love: failing to remind us that we heard more about Faulkner and Styron in the sixties than we did about Wright/ Ellington/Davis/ Ossie Dee combined.

(Start Rock n Rhythm and Mingus hymn clash, then become one.) (Repeat)

It was "Amos & Andy" updated we see each week. Never once did Coltrane have us view him live in color on ABCBNBC Coltrane was a casualty of the war in Vietnam, all of it in living/dead color on the ABCBNBC.

(Rock n Rhythm sung as a counter point is Mingus composition and lyrics.)
Rock n Rhythm Rock n Rhythm Rock n Rhythm Rock n Rhythm

BLOOD

Ornette Coleman and Don Cherry had no meals for their art.

CHOIR

But we supported Black art in the sixties/ seventies. Rock n Rhythm.

BLOOD

Yes, for 2 years, 3 months, 5 days, 11 hours, 8 seconds, 0.001. It was Faulkner-Styron's history that we learned.

CHOIR

But how were we to know? We ain't never had no history before. Rock nRhythm.

BLOOD:

Before Styron created Nat Turner.

CHOIR

Didn't we say, Mingus is dead! Didn't we, Mingus is Dead! Who? Charles Mingus. Rock n rhythm.

BLOOD

He dead, you know while we listened to the latest craze: Syn-the-tic Articificial Music.

CHIOR

What is Syn-the-tic Ar-ti-fi-cial Music? Rock n Rhythm (repeat)

BLOOD

Synthetic Artificial Music is artificially created/copied, electronically reproduced sound designed to simulate musical forms created/produced by beings of consciousness.

CHOIR

A copy of musical forms reproduced to sound like the music it intends to represent. Rock n Rhythm.

BLOOD

What do they call it? Do they call it the Gospel?

CHOIR

No! Rock n Rhythm (Repeat)

BLOOD

Do they call it, Blues?

CHOIR

No! Rock n Rhythm, Rock n Rhythm, Rock n Rhythm, Rock n Rhythm.

BLOOD

Do they call, Jazz? Rock n Rhythm, Rock n Rhythm

CHOIR

What's Jazz? No! Rock n Rhythm, Rock n Rhythm

BLOOD

Do they call it the Rhythm and Blues? Rock n Rhythm, Rock n Rhythm.

CHOIR

No! No! Rock n Rhythm. (Repeat)

BLOOD

Do they call it Country & Western? Rock n Rhythm.

CHOIR

Country & Western? Country & Western? Rock n Rhythm.

BLOOD

Do they call it Hill Billy? Rock n Rhythm.

CHOIR

Hill Billy, you mean Blue Grass? No! Rock n Rhythm.

BLOOD

Do they call it Rock & Roll? HUH? Rock n Rhythm.

CHOIR

Rock n Roll? Rock n Roll? Rock n Roll? Rock n Roll? No! Rock n Rhythm, Rock n Rhythm.

BLOOD

Do they call it Soul! Does it have Soul?

CHOIR

Rock n Roll?

BLOOD

No!

CHOIR

Blue Grass?

BLOOD

No!

CHOIR

Country & Western?

BLOOD

No!

CHOIR

Rhythm & Blues?

BLOOD

No!

CHOIR

Jazz?

BLOOD

Jazz? What's Jazz? No?

CHOIR

The Blues?

BLOOD

No!

CHOIR

The Gospel?

BLOOD

No!

CHOIR:

Then what do they call it? The Syn-the-tic Artifi-cial Music? What do they call it? SAM? SAM? Rock n Rhythm.

BLOOD

SAM? Not a bad idea! SAM! No, not SAM, DISCO! It's called Disco, Disturbing Interstitial Sounds Causes Depression.

CHOIR

Rock n Rhythm, Rock n Rhythm.

(Exit to applauds from audience)

Disco means Syn-the-tic Artificial Music: Disco SAM, Disco DAM, Rock n Rhythm, Rock n Rhythm, Disco SAM, Rock n Rhythm, Disco Sam, Rock n Rhythm, (Repeat)

(Audience is wondering what /who next? Whoo-we!)

CARETAKER

I find your question – Mr. Moderator – very timely. And for that, in the name of our ancestor and the creator we thank you.

And, you, Prof. Torts, your legal reasoning is obviously of superior quality. You are well grounded in the logic of western civilization.

Blood, I always knew you were talented, but I never would have thought to give that kind of response. Brilliant! And the chorus…. (Shaking Head, "unbelievable")

Anyway, while listening I had plenty of time to meditate. Coming out of meditation, it was revealed to me that although Prof. Torts was well versed in the philosophy of private property: and Blood in the logic of oppression, that is not our way.

Neither represented a response I could be satisfied in giving. No, that is not how I should respond to the question regarding birth rights, culture, and distinction. You see, in our document, The Hau De No Sau Nee, a Basic Call to Consciousness: Address to the Western World, Geneva, Switzerland, autumn, 1977, states that the The Hau De No Sau Nee have no concept of private property…….

"Before the colonists came, we had no consciousness about a concept of commodities. Everything, even the things we make belong to the creators of life and are to be returned ceremonially, an in reality, to the owners. Our people live a simple life, one unencumbered by the need of endless material commodities. The fact is that their needs are easily met. It is also true that our means of distribution is an eminently fair process, one in which all of the people share in all the material wealth all of the time……"

" Ours was a wealthy society. No one suffered from want. All had the right to food, clothing, and shelter. All shared in the bounty of the spiritual ceremonies and the natural work no one stood in any material relationship of power over anyone else. No one could deny anyone access to the things they needed. All in all, before the colonists came, ours was a beautiful and rewarding way of life." So, for us, the native people of North America, the idea of birth right is synonymous with the Creator. One cannot exist without the other.

NARRATOR
(Obviously, no one came to the forum expecting to be a party to this encounter. I wonder if anyone brought a tape recorder?)

CARETAKER
That brings me to a rather strange document our ancestors have passed on from the time they discovered it. As the story is told, the Six Nations Iroquois Confederacy "scout" in reality a Hau de no sau nee team – was visiting some outposts of the Confederacy when a very unusual object was found. (As Caretaker pulls out the "unusual object", the audience looks, but with no great deal of attention or concern.)

I'd like to play this objects voice recorder, and let hear what my ancestors heard after they discovered it.

SMART ASS
When did they discover it? (With a sort of laughter in his voice.)

AUDIENCE:
HA! HA! HA!

CARETAKER
In sixteen twenty eight, your recorded time.

(Upon examining the document…..)

SMART ASS

Wait a minute. That's a late model tape recorder, from here it looks to be around 1984 when it came out. How can that be a tape recorder found 1628 when tape recorders were not made until the twentieth century. What kind of game you trying to run, brother man?

CARETAKER:

Hold on! You Americans must learn how too listen. You are too ready to shoot from the jump, as you put it. The inscription reads right on the label, made in South Africa, 1984, A.D., Polaroid.

SMART ASS

("You mean from the hip! (jump? HA!) ")

AUDIENCE

HA! HA! HA! HA! Polaroid makes cameras! You know, like the ones that take pictures of our African brothers and sisters in South Africa. The ones they carry with their pass-ports. Man you way off. That's today! I don't know what's on it, but you just picked that up recently. Now, you/it may have some heavy things to say, but why the trickery?

CARETAKER

Look at it yourselves? (Beyond their wildest imagination.) (As we watch the image, a woman is speaking.)

AZANIA

They destroyed nature's calendar…. Why am I treated so bad? Tell me! Is this the nature of people from western civilization? They destroyed nature's calendar.

(Now from 3rd person to 1st and 2nd.)

You have given me your name and number, a "passbook", you call it. Yet, I live like a refugee at home. At home, I'm treated like an alien. At home, I'm alienated. At Home!

(Caretaker interjects comment while someone makes an inaudible statement.)

CARETAKER

Someone said, "What's western civilization?", right in the middle of her statement. We never figured out how that got on the tape. (Tape: rewinds)

UNKNOWN VOICE:

……..At Home! What's western civilization?

URBAN CHORUS

Take it to the streets, take it to the streets.
(Images are now of whatever is mentioned.)
Rock n Rhythm (Repeat)

AZANIA

I'm human! I have distinguishable features – if that's important to you – a face, feelings, desires, a culture, a collective will: We are universal! No need to say, too. Desires are universal. Greed is vengeful. Nature's desire is universal. Man's desire is universal. Man's selfishness is self annihilation.

STREAMS

Take it to the streets. Take it to the streets.

U.C.

Rock n Rhythm. (Repeat)

UNKNOWN VOICE

What is western civilization?

AZANIA

Does nature desire that human's extermination be fulfilled? Is that nature's desire? I wonder what argument provides the best logic for self annihilation? Is it a sense of denial or a desire for recognition that has thrown us out of balance?

STREAMS

Tell us a lie
Do or dieROCK
Say bye, byeN(REPEAT)
Why should we tryRHYTHM
That's why our cry

AZANIA

Red or blue? What is the difference?

STREAMS

The Dreams Alive. Dreams never die. Rock n Rhythm, Rock n Rhythm.

AZANIA

A cry in the night the end is com……….

STREAMS

A cry in the night
The end is in sight
A perfect laser flight
But dreams never die
Their beginning is in the eye.
Rock n Rhythm, Rock n Rhythm

AZANIA

But tell me, what is our love? Love of peace?
Love of dream? Love of life? Love of desire?
Desire death? Do we desire death?

STREAMS

The dreams alive, long live the dreams.
AAAAH!   AAAAH!
The dream's alive, dreams never……

Rock n Rhythm

AZANIA

Believe? Is heaven beyond our dreams realized?
Are we there, yet? Are we there? So soon? By whose judgement?

STREAMS

Is that it?(Rock n Rhythm)
Is it there?(Rock n Rhythm)
Is it there?(Rock n Rhythm)

AZANIA

Outlaws! Space Bandits! 1984, Par Excellence. Star Wars Forever, Kimberley Mines, Citicorp, GM, ITT, IBM, ICBM, USA, SCBM, USSR, BMENS, USA, - Union of South Africa! Red or Blue?

What's the difference when the life ending forces threaten to deny the human will/ recognition as living, breathing intellectual beings?

Well, what's the difference? I've put a question ON THE FLOOR.
Have we been consuming too much? Intellectual beings, has there been too much food for thought?
Greed! Is it greed? Insecurity about never having enough? Well, is that it?

UNKNOWN VOICE

What is western civilization?

(Although speaker in the video letter cannot hear the other questioner, she appears to raise her question right on time.)

AZANIA

I don't know, would pride drive such a hard bargain. Whereby red or blue really makes no difference in pride and greed, are they opposites?

Is that why I'm treated so bad? Is that the key?
Do the absurd simply to keep "our" competition from doing it first? Is that the key?

UNKNOWN VOICE

What is western civilization?

STREAMS

Perrier is Mother Earth's first soft drink. Drink soft drink.

U.C.

drink soft drink. Rock n Rhythm.

AZANIA

Tarzan is dead! Yet (Pause) amazingly Africa (Pause) we (Pause) are alive. It is at great expense. The suffering and pain of my people have become unbearable! Heavy suffering! Great pain! The death, theft, and a rape are beyond imagination. Our imagination! So, I know you're not surprised we're not doing too well.

(Understated)

Twenty four countries are facing starvation, and this use to be a land-o-plenty. The western countries act like everything's okay.

URBAN CHORUS

Everything's okay.(Rock n Rhythm)
Don't you say.(Rock n Rhythm)
Everything's okay.(Rock n Rhythm)
We have our way.(Rock n Rhythm)
Everything's okay.(Rock n Rhythm)

AZANIA

Tarzan is dead! Cowboys run America. I know its not forever, but how does it feel to be free?

Two countries with enough weapons to destroy forever, for us. And, now I understand that my oppressors have one, too. They say life couldn't have been better, for us.

(Pause)

By the way, did I say those countries are in Africa, the ones starving? No home grown food! You get the drift? No home grown food. None. STARVATION!

But, what can we do? Our land is all through? Can we do for ourselves? Can we do what others avoid so easily while they tell us "violence is not the way to freedom? While death squads go about killing at will." Whom so they kill? Subversives!

URBAN CHORUS

Take it to the street! Why should you care? Take it to the streets! You are not there. (Rock n Rhythm)

AZANIA

Why should you care? Why should you? Can you say, without giving it a second thought, I want to free humankind from our oppressive tendencies whatever they may be? I want to further human understanding.

What ever else we do in life, I want to add value to or enlightenment. Can you say that without a second thought? Without looking over your shoulder, so the speak?

(Pause)

Is a nuclear bomb going to further human understanding? Will this be our unique contribution to nature's movement? Can't we wait for the sun? It may die in time. (Change) The future is under our care only when we learn what has meaning: learn that truth may be, but when it has no meaning to those expected of believe it, that truth is unto itself an abstraction. (Pause) But that's not the least of our problems, since our understanding of events can differ so greatly when you see my account of what happened, you should be aware that it may differ as greatly from any other account as March differs from December. Whatever!

Remember, my reflections of what happened are the reflections of what happened are the reflections of the victim: Theirs, the conqueror.............since our understanding of events will/can differ so greatly, our dilemma is how to act correctly.

UNKNOWN VOICE

What's western civilization?

STREAMS

Take it to the street! First strike ability. Take it to the street. You got mobility. (Rock n Rhythm, Rock n Rhythm, Rock n Rhythm, Rock n Rhythm)

AZANIA:Our dilemma? Un/re/doing ourselves. That's HARD! Death is easy. It's living that is causing us so much strife, Pain.......

It's inevitable! Why not end the process – living by exploding the final solution to every living soul, and see where that event will place us in space – time.

Why not?

I DEFY NATURE! Say it, I DEFY NATURE! Our beginning seems a good one.

Look, when it's normal for urban dwellers to expect people in rural countries to feed us and starve themselves, redoing the self is hard. VERY HARD!

Can you imagine if we were boycotted by the producers of food? All of us?

What a contradiction? So, why not? Why not end it all now? As an anti-life argument, it seems logical, does it not?

Tarzan is Dead! And, the Redskins are in the Super Bowl, again. Beaten! Same people! "Savages!"

By the way, where are the Red people who once were the caretakers of this land named in honor of liberty?

NARRATOR

(God Bless America)

UNKNOWN VOICE

[It's their dream that kept us alive. What's a Redskin?)

STREAMS

The Dream's Alive!
The Dream's Alive!
Rock n Rhythm, Rock n Rhythm, Rock n Rhythm, Rock n Rhythm, Rock n Rhythm, Rock n Rhythm.

AZANIA

If the eternal flame is our claim, if the sun has cooked your brain, excuse me, if the sun is our worship, can we not learn a very simple lesson from those who long ago converted conflagration into a ritual of the "Sun God"? Such a simple lesson! Native people of the western hemisphere, do you think you can teach them the dance so you don't have to go through this trauma of the new world civilization?

STREAMS

This ain't no jive.

URBAN CHORUS

The Dream's Alive
When The Clock Strikes Five
Give yourself a Treat
Dance to the Beat.

Dance to the Beat.

Rock n Rhythm, Rock n Rhythm, Rock n Rhythm, Rock n Rhythm, Rock n Rhythm, Rock n Rhythm.

UNKNOWN VOICE

What's a Redskin?
Where's The New World?
What's Western Civilization?
(The audience is now dumbfounded. Is this……)

PROF. TORT

Folly! Pure Folly!
(The audience response is quick.)

BLOOD:

NO! Wait! The speaker here was excellent! She started me to thinking, so I forget I was here. But I was referring to how they told us things would be better for us. All we had to do was adopt the ways of the new world.

CARETAKER

For them, it was nothing. For us, we gave up everything. I guess it seemed so easy because our culture was integrated. Everything interacted. They simple divided…… Yes, I know exactly what you mean. Everything related to nature's process of growth and development. We weren't competing with anyone or anything. Nature's environment was not an enemy we had to compete with; anything we had to subdue. Conquer! Destroy! Do you know the American has wasted more of nature's resources than…..?

STREAMS

…….The law allows, if I may interject. The problem is, some of us – those in control, let's say for the moment – do not agree with those communistic notions.

CARETAKER:

Communistic is to live in harmony? And, we should oppose that/ To live in harmony with nature – as intellectual beings ought to be capable of - is the sin? Is that the sin? A U.S. Secretary of Interior said that the "American Indians failed/ died because they practiced socialism." Is that our sin? Oh! No! I don't believe that! If that's the sin? Where do we begin? If that's the sin, were does life begin?

STREAMS

Look, we have more people living at the highest standard.

UNKNOWN VOICE

Possible. More than at any other time.

CARETAKER

I maintain that your statement is incorrect. We had the highest standard of living. We consciously did not need technology to find our spirituality. We followed nature's signals, her patterns, her movements. Everything had a balance.

ARLENE

Where humans given the responsibility of completing this phase of nature's movement?

MODERATOR
You mean "were"?

ARLENE
I said "were," What did I say?

BLOOD
I said, "where".

PROF. TORTS
I'm not sure I understand your question.

MODERATOR
I think she means.........

ARLENE
I am capable of saying what I mean.

MODERATOR
I was only...........

ARLENE
And, I appreciate that. But, I am capable of explaining what I mean. My question is simply this. What if the universe is so constructed that along the way something is always set in motion to trigger another process? You know like the going and coming of events? And, what if we are that process?

PROF. TORTS
Pre-destiny!

ARLENE
Are we predestined to make earth uninhabitable? Is that our role? Should we allow them to continue making bombs? Why should I bother to work? You're gonna blow the whole place up anyway.

BLOOD
Right on sister!

PROF. TORTS
Obviously I cannot answer all of those questions – you were talking to me, weren't you. All of you.......

ARLENE
........It's directed toward everything.......

PROF. TORTS
.......seen to have chosen me as tonight's target. So I'll respond to the best of my ability. The world is just not that simple anymore, if it ever were.

ARLENE
So what is the meaning of Birth Right? That seems to be why we're here anyway. Some of us, that is.

BLOOD

It means that all of us have a right to the value of our product. Human labor is required of us – even when the labor results in the creation of artificial intelligence – as intellectual beings, our minds and bodies function best when we are active. Nature gave us the space, ingredients, and ability to construct our own realities, erect our own restrictions, manifest our own dreams, annihilate our own selves. That's our right from birth.

PROF. TORTS

You believe in free will!

BLOOD

I believe we were given the things ABOVE. How we construct, use, apply, destroy is our business. Our contradiction. The urge in Western man – the American leadership- is to test nature; disrupt it completely and totally to see what will happen to humankind. I can go it alone!

ARLENE

That seems kind of crazy to me.

BLOOD

Death Wish!

STREAMS

Death wish. Death wish. Death wish. Death wish.

URBAN CHORUS

(Repeat while other half on loud speaker speaks.)

Better Dead than Red
Better Lead than Bread
Better Said than Dread
(Repeat)

PROF. TORTS

I say folly to you, you old boy. The modern world, or, the west, if you will, only wants to exploit nature's resources to help us realize our potential. That's what it's there for. Our use. We are not the only beings nature created to use tools, but logical progression says that the more we learn, the more we know. The more we know, the more complex our systems become the more materials we need.

CARETAKER

Technology! You left out technology.

PROF. TORTS

I see no need to mention it because this is not what we are arguing about. Birth right, and before that learning were the basis of our discussion. I was not aware that it had become a discussion on technology. I said materials.

ARLENE

How can you talk about birth right and not discuss technology? Didn't the white man use the gun as his most effective invention for acquiring land? Is that not correct? Is that technology?

PROF. TORTS

That might be true, but we want to live, too. We are not interested in destroy......

(At that point Poet Said Saud begins.......)

PROF. TORTS

......I said materials!

POET SAID

.....I use to meditate (is how Poet Said begins. Then he follows with) Now, I just sit and stare at reality.

UNKNOWN VOICE

(There it went!)

POET SAID

I use to search for meaning. Now, I just walk around aimlessly.

(Unknown Voice: Where am I?) I use to cry out, give me liberty, I want to let I be, all of us are equal and free. Turn off that learning tree.

STREAMS

(Unknown Voice: What happened?) Now, I just say, give me a cup of tea, I want to sit on your knee, all of us are alien to thee, TURN ON THAT LEARNING TREE, WHY ARE WE ALIEN TO THEE?

WHY ARE WE ALIEN TO WE?

(Arlene is transformed into Mother Earth as she begins to speak, but only after she has been "moved" during the reading of Poet Said.)

POET SAID

I wasn't going to comment except by way of question, but after giving it some thought, I've decided to speak my peace. It's been some time, now, since I've had a forum from which to speak.

Since man, and I say man specifically – assumed direct responsibility and claimed direct dependency from the Creator, he also claimed to be the original recipient of "God's work." As the original recipient of God's word, man's responsibility thus became – that of caretaker of this Earth. As caretaker, man thereby given power of attorney status and all of the rights and privileges invested in such status.

Man, under this arrangement, obviously could claim not only direct dependency and responsibility, but also the original position itself, by way of power of attorney. As surrogate, man assumed it was his role to speak for and to God. Man therefore becomes God's spokesman, interpreter, executor, and confidante. What an enormous responsibility invested in one fraction – minute fraction – minute fraction – of "God's" creations. Man alone was given the responsibility to govern this earth. Only man could decide how much when. He could even decide what.

But what was to be the "checks and balance"? Who was to maintain the equilibrium? Regulate the ecology? Advise man?

God! Yes, no one else but God. Only God could speak to man from a position of authority. Only man could talk to God.

Somehow in building this equation, man seems to have created a myth: AN ILLUSION of a lost imagination, if you will.

Whether one relies on logic or truth, the question must be the same, did the creator give man complete self retaliating power over this Earth? Or, was the evolution of intellectual beings simply an occurrence that neither signaled man's superior status or unique relationship to "God"?

(Streams appear dressed in white.)

STREAMS
Abuse Mother Earth,
Destroy Nature's Life.
Abuse our land,
Destroy nature's breath.
Abuse the spirit,
Destroy life's soul.
Abuse yourself,
And, now is forever.
Why not, end now forever?
Now is forever
End all forever (repeat last two lines)
(Streams disappear, Mother Earth returns.)

MOTHER EARTH
It may very well be true that man's universe is billions of years old – a highly understated proposition – but does that give man the right to conclude human life within its infancy?

Who gave man that right? His own intellect? Man simply thought of it all by himself? (Observation)

Power of attorney status – even if it were given to man alone – and, I repeat MAN ALONE – does not grant man the right to destroy his own life, other forms of existence.

Let's be real, would the all knowing creator place all, or some creations under the jurisdiction of a self destructive infant? Under a boogooloo wobbeling set of beings, who when they are told by me to stop – continue their destructive path? Am I, Mother Earth, to end up like all of the other parts of man's universe? Destroyed! Lifeless! Barren!

Look, all around you. Look! Lifeless! Barren!

No one there!

STREAMS
White Boi, White Boi, Where are you coming from?
White Boi, White Boi, Where are we goin?
White Boi, White Boi, Where are you come in from?
Where do we belong?

Is this earth not kind enough! A kind enough place? To house every living thing that come from/to Mother Earth's space.

MOTHER EARTH

Do you realize how much time – space it took to build an equation that would allow life to evolve in its many manifestations? All in one setting? There was no "survival of the fittest," here. Everything had a checks and balance, rhythm, harmony, form, time, space, movement.

Do you understand what it took to create such a balance: one, and many evolving constituents? Complimenting each others rhythm? Simultaneously? Look, what it amounts to is this, since the advent of western civilization, you have destroyed life's forces not one by one, but in droves and droves, in perpetuity; beyond anything measureable by the manual of creation. Is it greed? I don't know, but it's coming down to something's gotta give, you know what I mean? I've sat back and observed you human life, or other forms of existence.

Let's be real, would the all knowing creator place all, or some creations under the jurisdiction of a self destructive infant? Under a boogooloo wobbeling set of beings, who when they are told by me to stop – continue their destructive path? Am I, Mother Earth, to end up like all of the other parts of man's universe? Destroyed! Lifeless! Barren!

Look, all around you. Look! Lifeless! Barren! No one there!

STREAMS

White Boi, White Boi, Where are you coming from?
White Boi, White Boi, Where are we goin?
White Boi, White Boi, Where are you come in from?
Where do we belong?
Is this Earth not kind enough! A kind enough place? To house every living thing that come from/to Mother Earth's space.

MOTHER EARTH

Do you realize how much time – space it took to build an equation that would allow life to evolve in its many manifestations? All in one setting? There was no "survival of the fittest," here. Everything had a checks and balance, rhythm, harmony, form, time, space, movement.

Do you understand what it took to create such a balance: one, and many evolving constituents? Complimenting each others rhythm? Simultaneously? Look, what it amounts to is this, since the advent of western civilization, you have destroyed life's forces not one by one, but in droves and droves, in perpetuity; beyond anything measurable by the manual of creation. Is it greed? I don't know, but it's coming down to something's gotta give, you know what I mean? I've sat back and observed you destroy – no kill – thousands upon thousands of life's species: Birds, plants, people, bison, you name it. You didn't care. If it served your purpose……..

STREAMS

……….If it serves your purposes, you know what to do, kill it. If it serves your purpose, you know what to do, take it.

If it serves your purpose, you know what to do, experiment with it. If it serves your purpose, you know what to do, you know what to do!

MOTHER EARTH

If it, (Pause) if it were not me – I can be selfish, too – you are abusing and destroying, some of the things you have done are simply unbelievable. Simply unbelievable! For instance, why would you destroy billions of square feet of timber and then turn around and build a park in memory of someone who has more often than not taken life, human, and/or otherwise.

Unbelievable!

You killed people who were already building a vast reservoir of nature's logic and rebuilding process. Then you had to build a Botanic Garden to relearn what you destroyed. How many in Europe alone! Two million? Is that overstated?

And, in the process, as your reward, you became the medical doctor, medicine man, health control agent. Brilliant! You are still searching for the secrets. Look, they are right here. Look all around you. Secrets!

STREAMS
But the bush is gone. So are the trees. The birds. Oh such beautiful birds. Where are my beautiful birds?

MOTHER EARTH
You do not make life, not yet. You only reproduce it. No matter the form you discover, it simply allows you to reproduce it many different ways.

But you haven't discovered the secret of making my beautiful birds. Want my birds back. And, I want my trees, my life......You know what I'm talking about.

You must remember all life is important to me. So what did you suppose that I graded life according to superior – inferior distinctions? I make no distinction between human life and other life forms. That's your illusion. That's your image creation. You were granted the mind to think.

My life is of and from me, and the sun of course. (All praise (s) to our sun and the moon.) Without me there is no you, for now.

So if you plan to move on, move on! Don't kill life here then run. Is that to be your contribution to "the universe"? Must you be so crude? So destructive?

Is, hell you calling? Remember your bombs? Interestingly, you have so many ways to kill this earth. So many! I bet you don't get a chance to discover all of them.

(Streams enter walk toward audience and say)

STREAMS
Wanna bet? Anybody wanna bet?

(Ad lib, Repeat only if necessary, i.e. to make the point, point much clearer.)

MOTHER EARTH
You see, that is the logic of the perfect lie. Keep lying (rationalizing), and you'll destroy yourselves before you find the antidote to death. Your greatest dream. Life! Your greatest nightmare, death!

Now, wait-a-minute, I am not proposing apocalypse, you are.

(Speaking for Mother Earth)

STREAMS
I didn't make the bombs, you did. Are you for real? You mean there's no hope except through building more bombs? What logic – the perfect lie. Brilliant. Simply brilliant! Mad, but brilliant as D.Q. would say. Such logic. Anti-logic.

DOUBTY

Don't you think you are ex.........

MOTHER EARTH

......STOP!Don't even try it! Do you know now long the list is, don't even try it. Don't get me angry.

DON'T MAKE ME ANGRY. Up to now I've been rather patient. Too patient! Don't make me angry.

For those improprieties will be longer than the last ice age next time. You want to live in hell, I'll let you live in hell.

BLOOD

Another way to look at it is we've been here over three million years and three million years is three million years.

SMART ASS

Five million years. Man, where you been? Its five million years since the first homo-sapiens was discovered in Africa. And knowing the white man, I'd add another ten million years, and still think I'm too low.

FRANKIE

Now that's dumb! Mother Earth, or A.P. – whoever it is – just told Prof. Torts that his shit ain't gon work, how you think you can get away with some rank shit like that.

MOTHER EARTH

People! People! Just be quiet, and listen. O.K.?

DOUBTY

Well, you certainly don't have any faith in us do you?

MOTHER EARTH

On the contrary, it is because you have chosen such a dangerous path that I find it necessary to say these harsh things.

When I spoke with a non-threatening voice, you refused to hear me. Now you tell me I am being too harsh.

You never cease to amaze me. You always want it both ways. All the time. My, how selfish! I'll give it to you both ways.

DOUBTY

Yes, but how can we get ahead when you say all of these negative things about us.

(After hearing the complete discourse, Prof. Torts now offers)

PROF. TORTS

We need new explanations.

DOUBTY

What was that?

PROF. TORTS

We need new explanations about the new technology, and how it affects the dynamics of our emerging world. Our old answers simply will not work in tomorrow's new world.

DOUBTY

I'm now sure I follow you, please explain.

PROF. TORTS

Well it's very simple. Each evolving order of things needs/requires new perceptions from the people expected to make that order work.

For about a decade now, we have been involved in the creation of a new world order.

MOTHER EARTH

We? Did I hear you say, we? We have been involved...........isn't that a bit exaggerated?

DOUBTY

Not really! Whether we are conscious of our actions or not, we have been involved.

PROF. TORTS

I agree with you, but I'd say it a bit differently. I'd say whether we are aware of what's happening or not, it's still happening. There are people consciously involved in the process, and there are those who are simply participating. Not consciously mind you.

MOTHER EARTH

And there are the fall outs.

PROF. TORTS

Yea, of course, there are always the fall outs. That's usually occurs because as I said, their participation is in spite of any awareness of what's going on around them.

DOUBTY

And, you call there people, "fall outs"? Why are they fall outs?

MOTHER EARTH

Because there is nothing for them to do. The new system does not offer these people anything, except hardship and suffering or, clerical work, and service jobs.

DOUBTY

Is that because of a lack of preparation?

PROF. TORTS

Yes, neither the new system – i.e. order – or people who suffer are prepared to receive the other.

DOUBTY

You mean the new system is not geared up to handle the new problems that may arise............

PROF. TORTS

........And, the people who are displaced by the changes too drastic, run seeking safety elsewhere, then there are those who become the other classes – sometimes called the underclass, at others, the lower class – meaning inferior.

In fact, they are the victims of change. Whatever else they turn out to be, they are the victims.

DOUBTY

Why are they victims? Or, as you put it, why are they the victims?

MOTHER EARTH

Usually because they are the least informed about what's going on?

DOUBTY

Why are they the least informed?

MOTHER EARTH

Their access to and use of information does not keep them informed about areas of change most likely to have a direct bearing on their future. (Repeat)

DOUBTY

The least informed!

MOTHER EARTH

Also, their level of understanding of the languages they need to know is usually so limited that they can sit and have the most important information broadcast directly to them and not hear a word said. In other words, 90% of the people who read that sentence don't understand it.

DOUBTY

You mean, they don't understand what it means?

PROF. TORTS

Exactly! They've never learned the other purposes of languages. Most of the words they hear they never bother to find out what they mean.

DOUBTY:

Why?

PROF. TORTS

Probably because we live in a tele-video world. We depend more on what we see than what we hear.

DOUBTY

That puts the average Joe at a major disadvantage, doesn't it?

MOTHER EARTH

That's an understatement. No one seems capable of teaching the consuming public how to learn from television. It's there in the stories, and most of the people I know miss the point because they did not critique the stories as literature courses in school. You remember, this line means that!

……..It was slow, but you learned the way words may be changed around to say the same thing, or something different. Whatever!

PROF. TORTS

And, many people – like the Blacks in America – Lose their birth right in the process.

DOUBTY

That is why we are here?

MOTHER EARTH

That's how we're here.

PEOT SAID

Mirror, mirror on the wall, This is no intentional call, but, now that you are in my sight, was the great move a necessary flight, one that should cause I to lose my birth right?

(To the mirror)

More than a half-a-century has passed, and may your infinite wisdom last. Less than another half to go, before you are a rare breed of the 20th century.

Minus your age, and we guess how long our musicians live.

Subtract from the life of a Black musician living in This America, and you'll give how long an African may live, if she's lucky.

So, do we count our blessings? Count our dollars?

MOTHER EARTH

Count your dollars. Is that all? IS THAT ALL?

(Pause)

The answer this generation gives will either remove our ancestor's lands from misery, or cause further turmoil and suffering.

(Change moods)

Ruin! As the old folks use to say, "They just ruined it."

But, whose fault is it? No fault, any more! Too far gone for that, now. Now we must act. Yes, act like rational intelligent human beings, just once in our lifetime.

Just once! (Pause) (Change)

So we all sat silently, listening while he played the music our souls unleashed.

We sat! And, listened! Can you hear? Can you hear?

SMART ASS

Power! That's why the powerful are rich. Money brings them power. Can you imagine owning a ranch that is one million acres big? Illusion? Illusion? Is this really an Illusion? Do I really own 1,000,000 acres of land? Do I really own all that is there? All that is out there?

Is this all? That I own?

POET SAID

Can you hear? Can you hear? Music of the night, beautiful, articulate, proud, lyrical, picturesque. Can you hear? Can you hear? The quiet giant played his music of the night. The crowd looked on/listened with awe.

Awh! Awh! Did you see/ hear him do that? Did you see that? Awh! Awh!

We actually dreamed our realities through his horn as he played his music. Did you hear that? (Pause)

Did you hear? Did you hear? Tell me, if you had three wishes, what would you ask for?

Now, tell me this, what would you be willing to do to earn you first wish? Remember, you may want to make your last wish first. There are no restrictions here.

CHORUS

What did he say? Did you hear that he said? Did he really say…….

POET SAID

However, whatever you wish you must show the process of obtaining it, and the challenge you expect to receive. Creativity is a premium.

SOLO

But who is the giant? Who is the quiet giant?

CHORUS

it's only '84 and we're already sayin "way back in "77". Do we know what happened way back in "77"?

SOLO

Can you remember?

CHORUS

Do you remember?

SOLO

What did he say when he blew such beautiful music, our music?

CHORUS

What did he say?

SOLO

Can you recall?

CHORUS

It's only '84, and we can't remember '77.

SOLO

Can you hear? Can you hear?

CHORUS

The cry of the people was for the love of peace, they just ruined it. They've ruined it. But, what do we know? What do we know? Another 12 million years to go. What do we do, now? What do we do, now? Just 12 million years to go. But what do we know?

MOTHER EARTH

It was a fall from grace. That's why the Black man has had to suffer so. He turned away from God. God don't like ugly.

Did you hear me, I said God don't like ugly.

Can I get a here, here?

CHORUS

HERE! HERE!

MOHTER EARTH

Hallaujah

CHORUS

What do we know? Ghettos in the ghetto, communities in communities, communities in the ghetto, ghetto in the community. (Repeat)

What do we know? What do we know? What do we know? Another 12 million years to go.

VELDA

And Allah patiently observes us all!

AUTHORITY

We believe in a policy of non-racialism. By that we mean, all members of society are considered equal. Thus we practice non-recognition of the races, so called. People are judged as individuals, not as members of a particular group. Therefore, we see no need for quotas and affirmative action. Everyone here has ;;;

SMART ASS

Although I agree with the sentiment of your statement, I find that I must disagree with your projection of what has happened to us as African American people. I'd be the first to announce that the policies over the last 16 years have caused a devastating effect on the lives of black folks. A fool can see that. But I would not be so bold as to say that it has destroyed us.

(Back stage – time pause)

CHORUS

Ghettos in the Ghetto. Communities in the ghetto. Communities in communities. Ghettos in the communities. (Repeat)

SMART ASS

Times is hard! But I wouldn't exactly say that we are defeated.

(Off stage – Time pause)

AUTHORITY

You may be sterilized, but you can't get an abortion on your own.

CHORUS

You may be sterilized, but you can't get an abortion on your own. (Repeat)

(Speaker continues, nothing said.)

SMART ASS

I come from a time when everything was in abundance.

CHORUS

He must have been around during the war.

SOLO

Which war?

CHORUS

Every war! Aren't things in abundance during the war?

SOLO

I don't know? What's a war?

CHORUS

What's a war?
Nothing but a toy.
A silly game of play.
That's a war.
(Acknowledge for first time)

SMART ASS

I come from a time – you can be silly, if you want to – when everything you needed was there. (Off stage – time pause)

CHORUS

Ask nothing of me, and everything will follow. Restrict me and nothing will be yours.

(Speaker continues, nothing said.)

SMART ASS

But, now looks like everything done disappeared. Right in front of our eyes.

(Enters stage)

PROF. TORTS:

You are looking at a new world. Things are different, now. Things have changed. Nothing stays the same. Not anymore. Things change!

MOTHER EARTH

That is true! But I hop you're not trying to rationalize turmoil and suffering.

You asked, what is a war?

SOLO

What is a war?

CHORUS

Nothing but a toy.

MOTHER EARTH

Nothing but a toy?

CHORUS

A silly game of ploy.

MOTHER EARTH

A GAME! War is a silly game? Is that your claim? That war is a game?

Do you mean like the Baltimore Orioles and the Dallas Cowboys?

CHORUS

Who has the claim?
The winners of the game.
The winners of the game.
Have the first claim.

MOTHER EARTH

I say there are no winners anymore.

CHORUS

That's your claim! Who says?

MOTHER EARTH

I say! Humanity says! It is not a game. Cowboys and injuns was not a game.

CHORUS

Sure it was. It was a war game.

MOTHER EARTH

I knew you'd finally show your hand. War is not a game.   And, if it is to you may God help you.

CHORUS

Then tell me why did ABCBNBC have instant replays of the war in Vietnam? Score: "30,000 Viet Kooks dead, 125,000 wounded over the past week. No American causalities reported." This is the third week no American causalities were reported.

The American Team seems to have a win streak going let's all say, "Go Boys". "Wipe um out, and get your asses back home where you belong."

MOTHER EARTH:

So who has the tapes? Where are the tapes? Are they at CBS or NBC or ABC or all networks three? Where are the tapes? Who has the tapes?

FIRST SOLO

What is the value in preserving your grandmother's letters, post cards, greetings, Bibles, furniture, books, scrapbooks, cookbooks, guilts, 78 RPM's, 45's, BLACK POSTCARDS! Black GREETINGS,.......?

SECOND SOLO

What is the value in making and preserving records/tapes by Guitar Slim?

AUDIENCE

Who is Guitar Slim?

FIRST SOLO

What is the value in videotaping the Haitian ART Exhibit at the Brooklyn Museum, a few years ago?

CHORUS

Was it taped? Was it taped?

SECOND SOLO

What is the value of a central audio-visual library service to those who might want to see something cultural, occasionally?

CHORUS

But, where are the tapes? Who has the tapes? Is it the CIA? Or, the Schomburg? The FBI or ERIC U?

CHORUS

Where are the tapes? Who has the tapes?

FIRST SOLO

Are they in the basement of the Smithsonian? On the streets of our lives moving each obstacle one by one, grain by grain.

CHORUS

But where do we find it? Where is it located, our culture!

SECOND SOLO

It is here? Is it there? Is it everywhere? Where is our culture?

CHORUS

Here! Look over there. It's Everywhere. Look to the North. Look to the South.
It's Everywhere. It's Everywhere. Look to the East. Look to the West.
It's Everywhere. It's Everywhere. Look over here. Look over there.
It's Everywhere. It's Everywhere.
(Another Movement)

FIRST SOLO

A flight through reality is sometimes often painful/joyful.

CHORUS

What do you say? What is today?

FIRST SOLO

What do we say? Make the pain go away. Make our pains go away.

SECOND

Give us joy today.

CHORUS

Joy is a painful way. Pain in a joyful way.

FIRST SOLO

I said give us joy today.

CHORUS

Joy in a painful day. Pain not a joyful day.

SECOND SOLO

We need some joy today.

CHORUS

Joy is painful today. Pain in joyful today.

FIRST SOLO

I need some joy today.

CHORUS

Please make our pains to away. Give us some joy each day.

BOTH SOLOS

I need some joy today. Give us our joy today.

CHORUS

Give us some joy each day. We have our joy we pray.

(Repeat)

SMART ASS

Gibran said, "knowledge is life with wings." What he didn't say was for us to accept its value it must be presented by the characters we identify with: A point intuitively understood by those who've read Jonathan Livingston Seagull. So tell me, do we call Bach a contemporary or a disciple of Gibran?

POET SAID

Twinkle, twinkle, twinkle star. How I've searched for you afar.
You seemed so near, but where you are, I cannot determine from this star.
I searched every night, By starship flight, Only to find you not by sight.

CHORUS

It's outa-sight, it outa-sight, not to be reached by starship flight.
It's outa-sight, it's outa sight, not to be found in a permanent night.

POET SAID

What to do. Since you're all gone. Should I stay here all alone?

CHORUS

All alone, you're all alone when the starship's gone, you're all alone.

POET SAID

12 million years to go. Don't you recall, I said there's only 12 million years to go.

CHORUS

What's 12 million years. For a starship flight. That can be done in a single night. A single night on a starship flight. That can be done at our dream's delight.

POET SAID

I pray you see us through our flight in search of you.

CHORUS

A single night, A perfect night. The only flight, on a perfect night.

POET SAID

I pray that is we fail our souls don't go to hell.

CHORUS

GO TO HELL. GO TO HELL. If you fail.

[Repeat in any

Arrangement you prefer.]

If you fail. If you fail, Go to HELL.

SOLO

Many eons to go for 26 to be no more. Even then 26 will come again.

CHORUS

You are my destiny. Please come and set I free. I am beholden to thee.

Am I your gift to be?

(Mother Earth enters unexpectedly speaking)

MOTHER EARTH

I have no problem with your search to discover. Your need to know, I find it a rather curios way to learn about your vast surroundings, as a matter-a-fact. My question is this, however, why must what you discover always be turned into a commodity for its value to be realized?

Why must wars be fought for you to test its value? Why must the (body/earth) from which you came be subjected to your urge to know how much you can take from it?

Again! Again! Again! And Again!

Why must you subjugate others in order to have a better material life? Is there something you have learned that I don't know! After all, I'm only Mother Earth. I can't possibly know all. Do you know more? Something else, maybe?

As I understand, we arranged things so that life could evolve/ continue from a number of possibilities. As things turned out, you were one of those possibilities: Sort-of-an-unknown.

You were always referred to as the unknown. The more you learned, the more you wanted to know. A rather interesting trait, we thought.

The truly fascinating thing about you was, the more you learned about how things are, the more you wanted to arrange them to meet your desires. I'm sure I don't have to quote any examples to make the point…….

……And, contrary to Western myth you don't abandon your "Man is the center
of the universe" thesis at all. You expanded it.

SMART ASS
We may turn out to be nothing but an unsuccessful experiment of intellectual beings operating on a continuum of free will/determinism or as you put it biologically, genetics v. environment. But isn't all the same?

BLOOD
If we fail, maybe the next time humans, or whatever, will be programmed to operate from another set of principles.

SMART ASS
Like the bees and ants?

BLOOD
Yeah! Something like that, wouldn't it be funny if we woke up one morning an all the roaches, bees, wasps, yellow jackets, and water bugs had put a quarantine around all of us.

You know, just like that!

ANT
All right you humans, we're tired of your shit, git off the pot…….don't move 'til we tell you. HA! HA! HA!

BLOOD
(To Audience) Just sit there and think about it for a while. You know what I mean? (Audience laughs) HA! (Now serious) Some how, if we don't find a solution, nature has built-in safeguards to protect itself. That's what I believe.

SMART ASS

Man may very well be on the verge of discovering "the beginning." The true Adam & Eve story, as it were – if I may be "proper" for a moment. He may very well learn how to clone "reproduce" uni-sexually, create an atom, or anything else you can imagine, but if he continues to use warfare as the most productive way of discovering the value of the atom, he may become an abstraction that is no longer attached to himself objectively or subjectively. In that case, the imagination of man will no longer be necessary because man will have become what he is trying to discover. AN ABSTRACTION! HA! HA!

MOTHER ARLENE

We must always remember that those who make the rules define reality.

(Chorus repeats slowly singing)

STREAMS

We must remember that those who make the rules define reality.
Lord. Lord. Lord. Lord. Lord. Lord.
(Response)
I said, Lord. Lord. Lord. Lord. Lord.

MOTHER ARLENE

Is that why training us – I know that this is awkward sounding but I must get it out before I forget my thought. Did you understand my question? Let me repeat it again. Is that why Black people are so slow to accept their own ancestors contributions to world culture? Even when they themselves inadvertently practice that same basic culture? Is that our problem, that is, we don't control our own reality?

STREAMS CHORUS

Lord. Lord. Lord. Lord. Lord. Lord. Lord.

(Response)

I said, Lord. Lord. Lord. Lord. Lord. Lord.

MOTHER ARLENE

Is that because when our reality is defined by someone else, both of us start to believe that only the person who defines, knows all the answers about what, when, and how the beginning happened?

STREAMS

I said, Lord. Lord. Lord. Lord. Lord. Lord.

MOTHER ARLENE

Sure, exactly. Those who solve the mystery of the beginning can claim the knowledge. Such a narrow focus causes the ones with the most technology to claim the most favored position. Through the power of the gun – faith is what they call it –we are made to believe that the claimant has earned exclusive right to the most favored position.

STREAMS

Lord. Lord. Lord. Lord. Lord. Give me faith Lord. I need faith Lord. I need faith.

(Response)

CHORUS

I said, Lord. Lord. Lord. Lord. Lord.

MOTHER ARLENE

(Transforms back into Mother Earth)

Of course when evidence is required, a simple referral to a written document will suffice.

STREAMS

Give me faith Lord. I need faith Lord. Lord. Lord. Lord. I need faith.

(Response)

CHORUS

I said, Lord. Lord. Lord. Lord. Lord. Lord.

MOTHER EARTH

(Mother Earth appears as Mother Arlene again)

….And, those credited with writing the document verifying their claim of the most favored position because they possess the document of verification. After all, they can explain the beginning. They are the beginning.

STREAMS

Through revelation or verification, I need faith. Lord. Lord. Lord. Lord. Lord.

Through revelation or verification, I need faith Lord. Give me faith Lord. I said….

MOTHER EARTH

There's, is the true word. The written word, as the keepers of knowledge and information! They are the providers of light, the interpreters of God in the image of man, the god, and the white man. Is that why black people fear their potential?

STREAMS

(Sing) Let me aim high, Lord. Through faith, let me aim high Lord. Give me faith Lord. By revelation or verification give me faith. I need faith Lord. Please, give me faith Lord. Lord. Lord. Lord. Lord.

SMART ASS

Do you remember how a famous athlete publically scolded Paul Robeson, the person responsible for him being in sports? Can you image an athlete chastising Paul?

STREAMS

Give me faith Lord. Please give me faith Lord. I need faith Lord. Please give me faith Lord. Lord. Lord. Lord. Lord.

(Response)

I said, Lord. Lord. Lord. Lord. Lord. Lord. Lord.

DOUBTY

We must remember that those who make the laws define our reality.

STREAMS

Lord. Lord. Lord. Lord. Lord. Lord. I said....

(Call and response)

AUDIENCE

Give me peace. We want peace. Give me peace. We want peace. Give me peace. We want peace.

AUTHORITY

Obviously a rebellion in the making. Ban this work. Ban it now. NOW!

STREAMS

Lord. Lord. Lord. Lord. Lord. Lord. I said....

AUDIENCE

Give me peace. We want peace.

AUTHORITY

These's a rebellion in the making. Banishing it. Banish it. A rebellion is in the making. Banish it. Banish it.

AUDIENCE

Give us peace Lord. Please give us some peace.

AUTHORITY

That's Communism.

STREAMS

Communism. Communism. That's called communism.

Communism.

(Response)

I said, Lord. Lord. Lord. Lord. Lord.

AUTHORITY

COMMUNISM. COMMUNISM. ALL OF THAT IS COMMUNISM. WHAT YOU SAY IS COMMUNISM. COMMUNISM.

STREAMS

NO IT'S FASCISM. FASCISM. I SAY FASCISM. FASCISM.

AUDIENCE

LORD. LORD. LORD. LORD. LORD. LORD. I SAID....

POET SAID

Mirror, mirror. Please forgive, but you are my only way out. With you it's revelation and reflection. With you, I can see myself.

MIRROR

Reflect!

STREAMS

Reflections reveal the object itself.

(Response)

Reflections reveal the subject as self.

AUDIENCE

In the year 2020 the meek shall inherit the earth.

(End simultaneously)(Build up to a soulful searching crescendo)

AUDIENCE/STREAMS

Lord. Lord. Lord. Lord. Lord. Lord.

(Hands are clapping. Body language shows spiritual up-lift-ment. But not a carnival.)

(Streams become background music to Smart Ass.)

SMART ASS

You want to know what the vote for Jesse's all about? (Pause) We look around, and what do we see? Everybody who was ahead of is moved up a notch or two after we made our demands for human rights in the 50's and 60's. And, we still got high unemployment, low paying jobs, bad health, poor education, and not shelter.

So, we say, if we have to we go to alone. It's really easy. We already vote as a block. Always have. All we need is to do now is increase the numbers.

We want Jesse. We want Jesse. If we don't win, we understand that. The point is, we don't loose. If we keep sticking together. Everything will be okay.

(Solo singer for Streams is pacing around stage in a sort of rhythmic fashion.)

STREAMS

(Sing) Don't we say, everything's okay.

(Response)

CHORUS

When it goes my way, everything's okay. Everything's okay when it goes my way.

(Fade off the stage) (Enters Moderator)

MODERATOR

WELL!

AUDIENCE

WELL!

(Great laughter of relief comes from the audience.)

MODERATOR

Well, obviously this is not what we had planned. This was not our planned format for the evening. Although it got dramatic for a while I hope it has cleared the air for us to move forward.

As you know, we began with a talk on learning by Professor Torts. Actually, we started with a poem by Mr. Said Saud. In any case, Professor Torts lecture on learning somehow led us into a rather spirited debate on a topic I have given a great deal of thought to: Birth rights.

Simply to repeat matters, I read a quote from Mr. Spencer-Brown the noted mathematician which said, "There can be no distinction without motive; and there can be no motive unless contents are seen to differ in value."

BLOOD

The question is, what are we going to do about it? Our right are violated; and like mother nature said....

AUDIENCE

MOTHER EARTH. MOTHER ARLENE. IT'S MOTHER EARTH.

BLOOD

Whatever! Anyway, remember Rockefeller at Attica? Ain't no way to justify (audience becomes uneasy with that reminder.)Ain't no way to justify killing all those bloods, and the guards too. Ain't no way in my book. These dudes in prison, where they goin' to? Huh? Where they goin' to. Tell me that. Like I said, know what the problem is**. What we gon' do 'bout it.

MOTHER ARLENE

Calm down. Calm down.

AUDIENCE

Chill out.

MOTHER ARLENE

Yea, chill out. As the young bloods like to say.

YOUNG BLOOD

Use to say. That's old.

MOTHER ARLENE

What's the latest?

BLOOD

Back to the same. You know, "cool it mother."

YOUNG BLOOD

HE DON'T KNOW WHAT HE'S TALKIN' ABOUT. (slap five and laugh)

MOTHER EARTH

WELL ANYWAY, I'M SURE THAT MY POINT WAS (voice lowers) understood just as well. Now, what were you saying Blood?

BLOOD
Oh! I'm through. I was finished.

MOTHER EARTH
Okay. Mr. Moderator. You were asking your question again. I believe we are still trying to understand birth rights as a principle. Is that correct?

MODERATOR
Yes, that is correct. I could not have said it any better. Not trying to be – auh! Where did you people come from? You have so much life. Energy. Determination.

MOTHER EARTH
Sir, I suggest that you quit while you are running ahead.

MODERATOR
Yes. I agree. Anyway my question was….

(Audience laughs)

….What is the basis for defining any given property or thing as having more value than another?

(Audience looks at each other in puzzlement.)

Is the amount of activity it tends to generate? The space it occupies?

(Audience still does not know what Moderator is asking.)

What is the basis for a particular class of individuals assuming the most favored position?

What distinguishes them from others, birthright?

Heritage? Name?

MOTHER EARTH
Name? What name?

MODERATOR
Like the Puritans! The founding fathers.
(Call)

STREAMS:
What 's in a name?
(Response)

The basis of a claim.
(Call)

The basis of a claim?
(Response)

That's what's in a name.

MODERATOR

George Washington! Abe Lincoln!

STREAMS

Birds of a feather flock together.

MODERATOR

Aren't those the names that made us free?

AUDIENCE

What's in a name?

STREAMS

Birds of a feather flock together.

AUDIENCE

The basis of our claim.

STREAMS

Birds of a feather flock together.

AUDIENCE

Is that why our name?

BLOOD

Are you trying to tell me that there was no revolutionary Black during the colonial wars of the Americas? Not even in these United States called America? Not even one?

STREAMS

Birds of a feather flock together.

AUDIENCE

What's in a name?

STREAMS

Birds of a feather flock together.

AUDIENCE

The basis of a claim.

STREAMS

Birds of a feather flock together.

AUDIENCE

The basis of a claim.

STREAMS

Birds of a feather flock together.

AUDIENCE

That's what's in a name.

STREAMS

Birds of a feather flock together.

MODERATOR

To answer your question, "what distinguishes the most favored from the rest of us," I'd like to quote from Mr. Spencer-Brown's Laws of Form. On page one, he said, "If a content is of value a name can be taken to indicate this value." Thus, the calling of the name can be identified with the value of the content.

BLOOD

So the name "Puritan" automatically gives that person the most favored position in America. Is that your point? So, who runs America? The Puritans.

MODERATOR

Yes, exactly! Obviously, the Puritans – or Pilgrams if you must – are valued more highly than other Americans, and that value can be identified with the calling of that name: Puritan.

STREAMS

"We take as given the idea of distinction and the idea of indication, and that we cannot make an indication without drawing a distinction. We take, therefore, the form of distinction for the form." (This passage is repeated over and over. At first slowly, with an increase in the pace as the repetition continues.)

(The Disunity Ensemble joins in repeating the same passage but with a different meaning intended. As they join in, it is a counter to the Streams repetition. Both are now repeating the same passage at counter time with different meanings. Antagonism runs high until it ends with both repeating the passage at the same time.)

(Streams chorus breaks out into a counter statement.)

CHORUS

IL-LUS-SION! IL-LUS-SION! IL-LUS-SION! IL-LUS-SION!

DISUNITY EMSEMBLE

You must indicate. Is that the motive? You must indicate. Is that the motive?

LEAD SINGER

With junk that we don't need. And, pills that make us bleed, we say,…..

CHORUS

Everything is okay. Everything is okay.

LEAD SINGER

I said with junk that makes us bleed and pills we don't need we say…..

CHORUS

Everything is okay. Everything is okay.

LEAD SINGER

Don't we say…..

CHORUS

Everything is okay. Everything is okay.

(Woman screams from audience)

LEAD SINGER

I said with junk that we don't need pills that make us bleed, we say….

CHORUS

Everything is okay. Everything is okay.

LEAD SINGER

Remember this is 1984, we've got 12 million years to go.

CHORUS

Everything is okay. Everything is okay. (Repeat sequence)

LEAD SINGER

Remember this is 1984 and 26 million is now 34. Yet we say….

CHORUS

Everything is okay.   Everything is okay. (repeat sequence)

LEAD SINGER

Do we now have another 8 befo we count the 12 we had befo.

CHORUS

Everything is okay. Everything is okay. It's only 1984 so what do we know? Another 12 million before 1 million years of atomic snow. One million years of atomic rain showers befo another 26 million years in a row.

LITTLE WONDER

Okay, I give up.

POET SAID

What do you mean, you give up? Give up what? Oh, you're talking about the poem….

AUDIENCE

The poem? I'm talking about the whole affair. The whole damn thing.

POET SAID

…The poem about 12 million years to go. You know what that's about.   —I'm really referring to the last one. It was an explanation of the first one I recited. HERE NOW AND THERE. Scientists say that the earth goes through a radical transformation every 26 million years. I think it begins with 1 million years of radiation showers, then earth begins the reconstruction process again. Or, something like that. I ain't no scientist, so I might have the facts wrong. You must admit that it is an interesting theory.

LITTLE WONDER
FOR ANOTHER 26 MILLION YEARS? Oh, sorry.   I didn't know that I was talking so loud. (Audience laughs, but watches this little wonder with interest.)

POET SAID
Yes! But what do we know? In '77 we had 26 million poor but now it's 84, and we have 34. But what do we know? Where do we do?

LITTLE WONDER
So, where does the number 12 come from?

POET SAID
I think it was some astro-physicists who said that 14 million years have passed, and we have 12 million to go.

AUDIENCE
So how are we suppose to know any of this? What are you sayin?

(Another member of audience shouts out, "Public radio. Magazines.")

AUDIENCE
So how do you do it?

POET SAID
Do what?

AUDIENCE
Use poetry to say what I ain't never heard before. How do you do that?

POET SAID
You know. This is 1984 with the final battle to go. So beware. Prepare with econofare. For the final battle on T.V. on NBC, May 6,7,8, 1984. Prime time.

STREAMS
MAY DAY! MAY DAY! Prepare for the final battle in living color brought to you by the sponsors of the 1984 Olympics in Los Angeles, California, U.S.A. MAY DAY! MAY DAY! Prepare for the final battle. MAY DAY! MAY DAY! (Repeat)

POET SAID
With only 12 years to go

and 26 million now 34

and the final battle in 84

although we have another 8 before

we count the 12 we have to go.

What do we know?

What do we know?

It's now 1984

But what do we know

Another 12 befo

1 million years of radiation showers

1 million years of radiation showers

Befo another 26 million in a row.

So what do we do, now?

In '77 we had 26 million po

Now it's 34 in 84

So what do we do, now?

What do we know?

STREAMS
(Begin singing) Everything is okay. (Repeat in a funcky spiritual blues vain)

LEAD SINGER
With junk we don't need. With pills that make us bleed. If we don't take heed, can we say? Everything is okay? Can we say....

CHORUS
Give me peace. We want peace. (Repeat)

RESPONSE
LORD! LORD! LORD! LORD! LORD! I SAID.....

(Streams become quiet as a new speaker stands to say his peace)

JAZZ MUSICIAN
You know, I really had not planned to delve into this matter of birth-right – especially as it relates to Black music – because it is so personal to our artists, so very personal to me as a musician. To put it bluntly, I must go to some where else simply to hear my music on record. You know what I mean? Simply to know my contributions I must purchase my music as a commodity.

ANNOYN
A good! It's called a good. What you purchased is either a good or a service. This commodity operates – is presented – as a good, service or entertainment. Which ever one you want you must purchase for a price. The question is where is the value of the product found? In it's creation? How is that determined?

These esoteric questions seem to bother me. This can take us so far away from what we are trying to learn, that I get disturbed when I hear one being raised.

(Audience looks at Annoying in disbelief)

JAZZ MUSICIAN

Oh, I agree totally. That's why I've tried to remain silent. You see, it's esoteric to other people. For me it's basic. Do I, or do, I not have a right to have immediate access to my creation as a commodity without having a mortgage placed on my past?

ANNOYIN

You mean, future.

JAZZ MUSICIAN

I mean past.

ANNOYN

So what is your question? I don't quite understand you.

(Audience laughs, "Is she serious?")

JAZZ MUSICIAN

My question is this. Do I have a right to preserve the music I created?

ANNOYN

Right? I'm not sure I can accept the word right as you are using it. "Privilege seems to be better suited for what you are talking about.

JAZZ MUSICIAN

Privilege? What privilege? What's privilege? An assumed right. Okay, privilege. Whatever. In that case, I so have the right to take the privilege and record what I create.

ANNOYN

No! You do not know?

JAZZ MUSICIAN

Then who does?

ANNOYN

It's rather complex.

JAZZ MUSICIAN

In what way? Complex in what way? Does the musician not have a right to have his or her music heard? Should there not be facilities to house our musicians so that they may work/ play their art and more than occasionally.

BOTHSIDES

…If they so desire. They may not want to sing or perform often. Or, have their music recorded.

JAZZ MUSICIAN

I agree. Whatever the arrangement might be, it should be designed to encourage creativity; and the preservation of our culture.

(Accepting J. M.'s thoughts. Both sides move the discussion further.)

BOTHSIDES

A musician should not have to wait until everyone goes to work during the day so that he can practice his instrument.

AUDIENCE: There are women musicians, too.

BOTHSIDES

Sorry about that. Arrangements might be made with public schools allowing the musicians to rehearse in their spaces if they will offer something in return like music lessons for a fee, of course. They might organize lab bands,… you know public service and creativity. Become a teacher.

(Member of audience tries to start a jingle only to have the rest boo her down.)

BOO BOO

Damn, can't even be creative around here.

(Audience laughs)

(Someone in the audience orders everyone to be silent. Old Lady enters stage.)

OLD LADY

Keep on playin'

AUDIENCE

What did she say?

OLD LADY

I said, keep on playin'. As long as you keep in playin' they can't take nothin' from you.

(Facing audience front and center)

Did you hear what I said? Yawl Thank you know everything nowadays. Don't you. You betta listen to me. You can't discount us simply because we's ole. (Old Lady moves slowly across stage as she speaks.) Wisdom! When knowledge is old wisdom is told. (Pause) Yawl Betta pay attention to the signs; read the Good Book; listen to Dr. King. He died for our sins. Don't let….

(Streams quietly assemble behind her)

(Verse)

STREAMS:

Our sins be his death in vain
he died for our sins
will we sin our sins again
or will we sin another sin
for our profits to die again

(Chorus)

Will our sins again be that sin
Will we sin that sin again

(Verse)

He died for our sins
Will we sin again and again
Will our sins again be that sin
Will we sin that sin again
Or will we sin another sin
For our prophets to die again.

(Chorus)

Will our sins again be that sin
Will we sin that sin again

(Verse)

If the king died for our sins
And yet we sin again
Will our sins contain that sin
Or will it be another sin
that take our prophets lives again

(Chorus)

Will our sins again be that sin
Will we sin that sin again
Will our prophets die as revenge
Because we committed anther fated sin

JAZZ MUSICIAN
Is our sin – that fatal sin – our failure to protect the birth right? Our culture – at times – can be so oppressive. At other times, we can appear so laid back; unconcerned about any thing, even those things that happen to us. We seem so unconcerned when our masters die.

BOTHSIDES
Yes, but what can we do about it? There's really nothing we can do.

JAZZ MUSICIAN
Except sin. Is that your point?

BOTHSIDES
The point is we don't have any real power in this society. None of us. Wouldn't you agree?

AUDIENCE
I agree.

GOFER
Well I don't. We have as much power as we choose to use.

AUDIENCE
Easier said than done.

BOTHSIDES

Yes, darn near impossible.

DOUBTY

The man ain't giving up shit. Not without a fight. He didn't rob and steal from everybody else because he planned to build a new land of milk and honey for everybody.

BLOOD

Damn sure didn't.

GOFER

I know! I know that. So, are you proposing that we lay down and die like hogs. Give up? Is that all we have to do? Completely give up?

BOTHSIDES

I didn't say that.

DOUBT:

Neither did I.

GOFER

Then what was your point?

(Old Lady enters stage again. Unexpectedly)

OLD LADY

SIMPLETONS! DON'T YOU CHILLUNS KNOW THAT IF YOU DON'T PRESERVE YOUR OWN CULTURE, YOU GIVE UP YOUR RIGHTS TO EVERYTHING?

(Pause) Don't yawl know that? (Complains as she leaves stage) Yawl don't never give up. Heritage. That's all yawl gots. And , it ain't got nothin' to do with you being Black. (Turns around – heads back.) You ain't po' 'cause you Black. You po' 'cause the white man don't care nothin' 'bout nobody 'cept hisself. He wanna spend his time scheme-ing on how he's gon' make his next kill. (Decides to return to center stage.) Then have the nerve to tell us he's doin' us a favor. Donin's us a favor.

(Disunity Ensemble takes up chant)

DISUNITY ENSEMBLE

     Create a new skill

On how to kill
Make the next kill
The best kill.

STREAMS

Give us peace. We want peace.
Give us peace. We want peace.

DISUNITY ENSEMBLE

Create a new skill

On how to kill
Make the next kill
A death kill.

STREAMS
Give us peace. We want peace.
Give us peace. We want peace.

FAITHFUL RADICAL
Biological warfare! Chemical warfare! Nuclear warfare.
What is it all for 'cept to kill.

STREAMS
Give us peace. We want peace.
Give us peace. We want peace.

DISUNITY EMSEMBLE
Create a new skill
On how to kill
Make the next kill
The final kill.

STREAMS
Give us peace. We want peace.
Give us peace. We want peace.

JAZZ MUSICIAN
Well, what's the point? Is it that our birth-right is not important enough to hold onto? Can you give up what you are born with without paying a heavy price? Can you do that without a heavy penalty? Can you do that without a heavy penalty being inflicted? On the individual and group simultaneously? I'll give you an example. Red Garland joined our ancestors the other day.

BOTHSIDES
What was that?

BLOOD
Red Garland is dead?

SMART ASS:
No he's not! He is? When did....?

BOTHSIDES
....Whose Red Garland?

JAZZ MUSICIAN

He passed on into the other world the other day in Dallas.

SMART ASS

Red Garland is a Jazz pianist whose greatest fame came while playing with Miles Davis.

JAZZ MUSICIAN

That was a very famous Jazz group at the time.

SMART ASS

The Miles Davis Quintet

BLOOD

Quartet, too.

DOUBTY

I've heard of Miles Davis, but never anything about, what's his name.

JAZZ MUSICIAN

Red Garland.

BLOOD

He died the other day.

JAZZ MUSICIAN

He's not dead. Hr lives in Dallas, Texas. The Masters of our music can't die. They live on in their music. Our music. They may move onto the beyond, but they don't....unless.

BOTHSIDES:Don't what? They don't do what?   Unless.

JAZZ MUSICIAN

...Don't record it., their is always that possibility that their works were never recorded. That is virtually a sin.

SMART ASS

You didn't say "die." She was listening for die.

JAZZ MUSICIAN

Thanks! "Die" unless we don't support them. There don't seem to be many roles for accomplished musicians any more.

BLOOD

Yea, it can get very lonely to you if nobody is listening to you when you're playin'. Kinda lonely out there in the beyond.

(Old lady enter front and center. Other actors move to the background.)

OLD LADY

Only a fool travels down blind's alley. Only those who don't know where their nakedness is seek protection from the clothin' of the flesh. Only those who become stagnant in their culture loose their birth-right. (Exit)

(Streams begin to chant in a loud whisper that is echoed.)

STREAMS
What was that? What was that? What was that? What was that?

(Return to discussion on birth-rights.)

SMART ASS
As I was saying, the death – or as Gofer said, "travel in to the beyond" – of Red Garland only points out how it is so easy for our musicians to enter the unknown simply by us forgetting the past without being dead.

FAITHFUL RADICAL
So he leaves behind the past. Leaving none of the present?

JAZZ MUSICIAN
No. No. We do that! The musician – Jazz/ Classical – musician remembers the past. Completes the circle. We forget to teach our offspring what it's all about. By the way Red Garland is not dead. He lives in Dallas, Texas.

(Poet enters)

POET SAID
Why is it so easy for our musicians to enter the unknown?

While, they leave behind all that is past?

Yet, leaving none of what they left present in our consciousness. (Pause. Reflection)

But it is only those who make that trip through the unknown who seem to reach immorality – in the beyond.

(Streams begin to chant in a loud whisper with echo.)

STREAMS
Is that so? Is that so? Is that so? Is that so?

LEAD SINGER
Is it so that those who travel through the unknown reach immorality in the beyond? So, what happens to the rest?

CHORUS
Of us? What's suppose to happen to the rest of us?

OLD LADY
Chil-lun remember only those who occupy the most favored position can claim control over all other's birth rights. They make the laws. Is that a lie? Caught you? (Pause) Didn't I ? if we believe that the only way we can git ahead is to act like those folks who have kept us down, then ain't nothin' good ever gon' happen to us. We'll always be left outta everything. Ain't nothin' good kin ever happen like that. You gotta believe in your self. If you ever gon' do anything in life, you gotta believe in yourself. Ain't no two ways 'bout it.

DOUBTY
Well? What are we suppose to do? What's goin to happen to us?

AUDIENCE

Well? What are we suppose to do? What's goin to happen to us?

AUDIENCE

PRAY! (Laughter)

MODERATOR

We'd better listen to Old Lady. What's she's telling us is basically true, you know! She completes the circle for us.

DOUBTY

What do you mean?

MODERATOR

You know? She pointed out so clearly how we indicate differences between each other. How we make distinctions.

FAITHFUL RADICAL

So did Mother Earth! She also said she is not taking any more of our self-destruction urges. She said she's tired.

BLOOD

Yea, what about caretaker? He rapped some heavy stuff too. You know! Came outta a whole different bag. Where'd he get that stuff from?

SMART ASS

And don't forget Blood. I didn't know the dude had it in 'em. That thing he did on Mingus was...Phew!

(Slap five)

DOUBTY

Yea, what was that joke he made about those insects?

SMART ASS

Oh yea! Something about, "we tired 'o yowl shit, git off de pot."

(Laughter—Slap five)

FAITHFUL RADICAL

....And, what about the Professor, Dr. Torts. He made some good points, too..(Someone in background)

AUDIENCE

...Always gotta have some liberal mudda fudda come talkin' some shit.

FAITHFUL RADICAL

Don't run that mess on me. What is right is right. Somebody's got to say it. And if my memory serves me correctly, if the poet had not led off with his poem you would have been up manure creek without a paddle.

(Pause. Reflection)

So, there is no need to be biased here.

AUDIENCE
RIGHT ON! Manure Creek?

(Professor Torts assumes podium)

PROF. TORTS
I'd like to thank all of you for such a stimulating evening. It was most fascinating. One I shall never forget. I also hope that I might have left some food for thought regarding learning as a process; and, what ever else I might have un-expectantly said. I enjoyed your "sit-in" you were quit a challenge.

ABDUL HAQMED
I know that some of you ain't gonne like it, but I gonna say it anyway. (Pause) what happened here tonight shows what can happen when you become "active" "stick together" "get involved."

Brother and sisters.

I don't care what nobody say, if we hadn't showed up things never would have turned out the way it did. As it turned out, a lot of issues got thrown out on the table. Things I most of never thought of before. I know I ain't never heard anything like that before in my life, except my great grand mother use to talk like that.

And, Mother Earth! Man! I don't know, where she came from…Phew! That was some heavy rap. In other words, the only reason tonight happened is we were here.

IMPATIENT
All right! We got the point. Let's go. I'm tired. I gots to work tomorrow.

ABDUL HAQMED
Come on, gimme a break.

POET SAID
As yawl get up to go home, I'd like to leave you with one last thought. You don't have to stop moving. But you have to listen. So, please listen.

AUDIENCE
SHHHHHH! SHHHHHH! Be quiet! Poet Said is about to say something. Go ahead Saa-eed.

POET SAID
Thank you, Brotherman, Sister woman!

Where you are
There might be a star
Whose light mightn't go far?
Not because it is not a star
Whose light can't shine far?
Is it because what you are?
Is who you are?
Do you think that what happened before?
Won't happen again? Think about it.

STREAMS

(In a repetitive manner.) Think about it. I say, Think about it. Think about it. What happened before will happen no more not as before not any more.

What happened before will be no more as it happened before not any more.

CHORUS

Let's draw a ring around a circle. Add in a cross. What do you see? Give it a name. Give it a claim. It's nothing but a game. Ain't nothing a game. Cause each is worth the same.

Each is the same. Ain't nothin' but a game.

(Audience begins leaving while singing is in progress. As chorus is completed, two citizens have a last word before they depart.)

CITIZEN I

You know, no one would think of us as people with a consciousness.

CITIZEN II

Yea, but you can't overstate that point. You're right. We do have a consciousness about us. Our feelings about each other are so mixed-up and confusing, however.

CITIZEN I

What do you mean?

CITIZEN II

Well, take tonight. If we hadn't been standing outside discussing politics, we never would have come to this lecture tonight. Never would we have heard the American Indians....

CITIZEN I

NATIVE AMERICAN! Indigenous Peoples!

CITIZEN II

Native people to the western hemisphere, what ever. Anyway, I never would have thought about them, not the way that Caretaker talked about them tonight. Would you?

CITIZEN I

No not really.

CITIZEN II

But our feelings are so shallow. We talk about the spiritual, but we don't seem to be able to transcend the physical and emotional parts of our lives.

CITIZEN I

I don't understand. And, it's getting late. What's your point? I got to go to work tomorrow.

CITIZEN II

I don't want to take up any more of your time, I know you're busy. Some other time, maybe.

CITIZEN I

NO! NO! Go ahead. I want to hear what you're saying.

CITIZEN II

We have the great distinction of calling ourselves people, how do you say it, people with a consciousness.

CITIZEN I

Being of consciousness.

CITIZEN II

Yes, that's it. Yet we — our feelings -- at our highest level of consciousness – have only experienced "living" on the physical and emotional plane. We are still unable to consciously enter other worlds without subjecting them to our narrow understanding of things and happenings. We are unable to stop for a moment and say, what does this world contain? You know what I mean?

CITIZEN I

Yes, I know, but that moderator said, we must make a distinction before we can identify – indicate – what it is we saw. Is that your point?

CITIZEN II

That's the point! We must always draw a distinction before we can indicate what we saw. So we go into a foreign culture, make our distinctions, and come out with a wrong interpretation of what we saw. That's such a contradiction.

CITIZEN I

OKAY. I understand. Now, I gotta go. See you later.

CITIZEN II

Yea, later. Thanks for listening.

The End

CRY OF MY PEOPLE
(On Birth Rights)

Act 1
Scene 1

POET SAID

She sat silently
Tears on her cheeks
Sorrow in her eyes
Joy long past
A long time ago
Overdue no more

Eons of pain
Sufferings of hardship
Ending life

Unending ……..

(Passing by is another speaker):

STREET MERCHANT
You wanna buy a stereo set, cheap? Hey, brother-man?

POET SAID
Unending,……..

(As a bystander):

CYNICA
Will it be this way all-the-time?

POET SAID
She sat silently

Tears in her eyes
Sorrow on her cheeks
Overdue joy
Long past
No more

Eons of pain
Suffering is hardship
Life ending
Unending…….

(Passerby speaks):

STREET BEGGAR

You gotta quarter you can spare, sister?

POET SAID

Unending now.......

(Bystander)

SCEPTICO

"Will my life be this way, all-the-time?"

(Citizen makes observation – lights Fade)

OLD LADY

Don't move so fast, that you don't know where you're goin.

(Voice of Streams choir singing) (Gospel style)

STREAMS

Freedom – we want freedom!
Freedom – give us our freedom!
Freedom – everybody wants freedom!

JABBO

I'm sorry, what did you say, just now? My mind was elsewhere. I only caught aglimpse of your – what you said. Everything happened too fast.

(Alluding to the poem, question & song)

OLD LADY

Don't move so fast that you don't see where you are headed, is what I said. You know people can get so caught up in what they are doin that they never find out what it is they (pause) do. The result is we go through life without ever realizing why.

JABBO

What prompted you to say that? It wasn't the poem we just heard.   That was about a woman, a sad woman or maybe it was about women in general, the oppression of women in general. But how did you tie it into your statement about life?

OLD LADY

I hadn't thought about it until you raised the question, but now that I think about it, it sounded more like those parables Jesus Christ was so famous for. He told great stories, I'm told.

JABBO

What so you mean?

OLD LADY

You remember those stories Christ told to make his point: That was the poet.

THOUGHTFUL SOUL

Interesting! I clearly forgot about that. I was thinking about King Solomon's works of art that were contained in the Holy Scriptures. So, maybe we are thinking along the same lines. Solomon was a poet.

JABBO

Wait! Wait! I'm lost! I really don't know what you two are talking about.

You've lost me.

JABBO'S FRIEND

Yea, me too. Long time ago.

THOUGHTFUL SOUL

Well, in the Holy Scriptures, Solomon is credited with writing parts of Psalms, Proverbs, and Songs. In hearing Christians discuss "Songs of Solomon", as they are called, it is obvious that most think Solomon was writing about a people's struggle, a people's suffering, longing.

JABBO'S FRIENDS

What are the personal loses?

STREET MERCHANT

A first claim based on Birth Right.

JABBO

What was that?

JABBO'S FRIEND

Can you repeat that, again?

OLD LADY

Birth Right! People's Birth Right!

JABBO'S FRIEND

Excuse me, but what the hell is Birth Right? And, how does that relate to the poet's poem about the lady. (Still unconvinced by the conversation up to this point).

(Spoken by the narrator, while players are visual) (Players can be seen talking)

NARRATOR

However, you must admit that the points raised have been interesting, so far. The question is what are they getting at. They keep raising these points I've never thought of before. It's almost embarrassing; I can hardly keep up with the conversation. Am I that far out of touch with my current events? Really, it's not even current events, it's more like poetry, literature, law, religion, philosophy, politics. Things I've never.... Yes, Politics! That catchall phrase for an unexplained event. You know, like they were fired from their positions because it's "political". Anyway, where am I?

NARRATOR

Why am I doing this? I seem to be trying to gain some sense of what's going on. I don't seem to have a grasp of what is happening, is what's going on is really what's going on.

(Right back to players as though they were talking/nothing has interrupted the process they were engaged in.)

JABBO

And, can someone tell me what's going on? Seems like a time lapse, but I don't remember anything (Pause) happening. You know the feeling?

JABBO'S FRIENDS

I know exactly what you mean. I felt all of these thoughts. Really, I thought I was talking to you, but somehow it seemed unreal. I can't remember what it was. This conversation seems so unreal. Black people do not have these kinds of conversation. This is not us. We don't have….. (Demonstration outside the hall can now be heard in full BLAST!)

REPORTER

The demonstrators are very awkward at this point because the demonstration was called at a moment's notice. The opposition? Prof. Torts, a very noted barrister in Great Britain before he became interested in the "Philosophy of Artificial Intelligence", has been invited to give a lecture at City Institute for the Study of Intellectual Development (CIF – SID!) on his new theory of intellectual development. "Yearning" Theory, as he calls it. Excuse me, viewers and listeners, one of the organizers of the demonstration is about to speak. Let's see who that is? Yes, it's Abdul Haqmed in the Kill Racist Coalition, pronounced KRACK, is about to take the podium. Abdul Haqmed!

(Dramatized like rally in African American community in1986) (Muslim greeting)

ABDUL HAQMED

Brothers and sisters and comrades I'd like to take the opportunity to thank yawl for coming out to protest this racist action today. As you know, today is the day of Respect! Everybody rise! Lower your heads!

(20 Seconds with "In a Silent Way" by Miles Davis Playing in the background)

Thank you! Thank you comrades, brothers and sisters. Why are we here today, I'm sure many of you are asking. Well, we just got word last night that Prof. Torts was invited to speak at the Important Hall, City Institute for the Study of Intellectual Development (CIF –SID).Who is Prof. Torts? Prof. Torts is ……………… (Interruption from Rally Participant.)

RALLY PARTICIPANTS

…… Hey man, cut the bullshit and let's get on with the show. I ain't here to hear no speech about no racist we already know.

(Streams enter as a "Greek" chorus – back up)

STREAMERS

Hey man cut the bull and let's get on with the show. I ain'there to hear no speech about no racist we already know.

(Rapid: One at a time)

What do you know? What do you know? What do you know?

(Haqmed catches on fast, makes necessary adjustment.)

Addresses Crowd –

HAQMED

I know we going to go into that lecture hall tonight and establish once and for all who has the right to the original position on this hemisphere, who has first right claim to the new world musical expression of New World culture. Ain't that right? (Feeling good about his conquest)

RALLY PARTICIPANTS

Right on, brother man! Say it again! Everybody didn't hear you!

(Confidence and enthusiasm) (Louder)

HAQMED

I said that we are going inside CIF –SID and determine who's boss. Is it we? Or, is it they?

(Satirical):

ALL STREAMERS

Is it we? Or, is they? Is it us? Or, is it them?

(Frustrated with the playful nature of the streams.)

RALLY PARTICIPANTS DON'T PLAY

Fuck that! That ain't no argument. "They or them", we know who he's talking about.

(FRUIT OF ISLAM move in to take 'DON'T PLAY' away from the crowd. Don't want any "agents" stirring up the crowd.)

STREAMERS

(Again, showing satire) (No condescension)

Is it we? Or, is it they? Is it us? Or, is it them?

RALLY PARTICIPANT DON'T PLAY

Who is he talking about? Man, who are these dudes? Where they come from? They friends of yours? If they don't shut up, I'm going to kick me some ass. This is serious business, We ain't got time for jiving around. Excuse me, Bullshit! You better take them dudes out-a here befo' I loose my kool.

STREAMERS

Chill out! Chill out!

(F.O. I. move to either side of DON'T PLAY just as he was about to move toward the STREAMS. Before surprise takes him, he is wisped out of the picture. Audience applaud.)

WHITE ACTIVIST SUPPORTER:

Yea, let's get on with the show.

(Demonstrators head into Important Hall to hear lecture. As demonstrators arrive, the lecture has not begun so they assume the stage to let their poet laureate "set the tone" for the evening's lecture.)

(Music heard behind the poet is a Randy Weston composition)

(Low reporters voice) (Again with Mike in hand)

REPORTER

The demonstrators have arrived before the lecture and have taken the initiative to allow one of their noted poets, Poet Said Saud read some of his "poetry" This is an uninvited reading I must inform you viewers and listeners. But, apparently a discussion has been held and, an agreement has been reached (Show parties arguing, then agreeing) between KRC pronounced KRACK, and the sponsors of the lecture, CIF – SID, the City Institute for the Study of Intellectual Development. Poet Said Saud is now heading toward the podium again. As you recall, he had been placed there only to be removed, and now he's back again. Let's see what Poet Saud has to say. Listening viewers, Poet Said Saud.

(Muslim greeting! Then Filler Buster)

POET SAID:

I'd like to thank you brothers and sisters and comrades for letting me come before you tonight. With such short notice, I thought I'd share with you one of my "Jazz" poems written for our immortal Randy Weston. I wrote this poem while sitting at the New Muse in Brooklyn, N.Y. Randy was giving a free concert for us bloods who can't afford to hear our music anymore. Yawls know what I mean. Right brothers and sisters!

(Audience response is positive) RIGHT ON!! (Pause – tone is set) (Slap five)

(Total Silence)

POET SAID:

What are they trying to tell us? I wondered, is it that we have no need to feel apart from each other? The drum hummed while a piano rang sounds of the African musical equation, our version, of course. The new was old was new again.   His idea was to communicate in a language about a force greater than our will to be.

(Randy Weston with Addison Weston on congas and Talib Kibwe on alto sax playing.)

The past was present! The future was here. A new voice was heard between the keys/impressions of a rhythm so often denied its place in the sun. It is, our sun I am referring. The one that contains the essence of our collective lives. Our united being. So? Where will we go next as we search around, in between, all about our own equation/definition of reality? What is our purpose for being?

(New thought enters) (Weston still playing)

POET SAID

The music played - he played for us - was the answer to our riddle: Is it possible to move at our speed with no history, and so much opposition? But, like a lost people, we are unable to see the Messenger, our prophet, when he performs right before us.

(Now, right to the question) (Weston still Playing!)

What are the problems of a people who are forever lost in their search for themselves? (Pause) To assure us that WE ARE ONE - that we are the ONES that – He came to communicate with, i.e., to talk to, if you will, to let us know that the sound was authentically REAL: There is a reality we can claim. There are rights to our birth! We can claim an original position, in the future new world.

(Description of Randy's Movement) – (Strong Weston now)

The Composer – our Messenger – moves forward as he goes back into our time, our space – you see, everybody has a space in this universe, on this earth – He combines our roots with each other: soldiering them, those severed roots buried in a foreign soil of human suffering, anger, pain, oppression, love ….. (Pause)

How can sound waves that are so near/How can voice sounds that are so dear – become so unreal to us?

(Dramatic) to our ears? (Pause when they are played back to us.) (Short pause) In time? By those among us who have bothered to search out our history where a search must be carried out? Where? Where? (Louder) (Answer) At home, of course!

Is it, we are afraid to know – to give – because to know – to give means we must know something about our suffering?

Is it, we really are not aware that mathematics and music evolved out of the same equation? Are related in time and space? As time and space?

Didn't we learn that the drum is universal – multi-versal in time and space? That it travels along the same electrometric waves as all other equations? That the drums taught us time? How to count? That our definitions of time/space can be heard through the rhythms of before? That the relativeness of things and properties is such that they are often expressed in the exactness of our multi-theme foundation?

POET SAID

(Speaking as a storyteller) A music (Pause) A people's music is an expression of their being; where they are –– How they are doing. A music that becomes mechanical reveals its separate-ness of from people. It shows a failure to appreciate what we all must know as we search—(Pause) a failure to appreciate what we all must know-- as we search out our destiny.

(Revelation) (Pause) But others know. They know the value of our music, so often, long before we have come to recognize its beauty. (Moderator gets anxious) (Audience is attentive)

So! They sit among us and listen, to hear, see, and eventually claim its value for themselves while we venture into new unexplored territories, evolving our creative labor, unaware of the connection between what we are trying to create and the necessary unity of a people's history.

So, as I said, others sit unannounced, unpretentiously listening, learning, trying to acquire the essence of what we take for granted…… (As though moving on) (Back to music) ….. The limitation of His instrument of creative labor and expression were under-stood, but he continues to push, press, out of frustration, out of a desire to make us hear, aware of how it all means one thing.

(A tone of frustration –but observation)

Somehow the instrument he played would not suffice, so he added a son with a drum – a more fluid instrument of creative labor: One more in tune with our verse – an instrument not of artificial creation – more organic – social – (Now referring to father and son) (Summary) And, they played together, as one. Then – the music began to flow forth as if – out of nowhere – No! - Everywhere …..

(Finished, applause, exit stage)

(The speaker for the evening, Prof. Torts, understands the dynamic that has gone down, so without introduction, he approaches the stage and podium. He moved "down front" when the demonstrators entered to get a better "seat" to see the action)

{Reporter enters, speaks quietly to the listening audience.}

REPORTER

……….. Listening viewers, apparently the guest lecturer, Prof. Torts, feels he needs no introduction because he has approached the podium unannounced. Let's hear what he has to say. (Fades out)

PROF. TORTS

I say poof, poof, to you!

(The unexpected statement cause unexpected reactions)

(And, he continues) (Audience laughs, then realizes he's the opposition. Immediate silence follows.) As a Barrister for the Queen, I found the demonstration very well staged. My "Hats off to you."(In a Cambridge accent) Let me say further, that I'd be a fool to try and compete with you. On the contrary, I shant fight with you at all.

I am here to engage in serious dialogue, as)(just before someone in audience was about to respond.) I see that you (Pause, looks right at the audience) are. However, (humorous) I must admit you caught me completely (embarrassing the moderator) by surprise, as I'm sure you did to our distinguished moderator.

(Audience laughs as moderator turns as red as a beet.) But I'm not a sore loser, and I love surprises that are well staged. Even if the aim is to disrupt my lecture. You see, it gives me more press. The more controversial I am especially if I did not orchestrate it – the more readers hear about me, the more books I sell. So, you see, you never know where a gift may come from.

(Laughter) (Not impressed)

PROF. TORTS

Okay, now for my lecture for the evening. I'd like to begin by thanking the City Institute for inviting me to your great institution, and allowing me to enter a format that will expose some of the ideas I've been pondering for the last twenty years. I welcome dialogue! Now, on with the lecture,

(Pause) with your kind permission, of course. If I can pick up from where the demonstrators began, I think the point is, learning is a multifaceted process that encompasses the ability to understand – comprehend – as a dialectical outgrowth of discovery, imagination, and observation: Learning combines the intellectual capacity to "think" with other senses operating within the physical realm of our existence, i.e., the human brain uses our ability to "think" to verify sub/objective reality in terms of our own existence, as reported by our senses.

In other words, in terms of the human equation – to use one of your terms – learning is an intellectual process that combines the energies of the brain – inclusive of the nervous system – in such a way that one is able to make some sense out of the "real" world. (Prof. Torts picks up speed in his delivery here)

So the world is as we perceive it to be, and it is not! It is what we learn that it is, and it is not. It is more, different, better, worse, etc., etc., depending on where you are in time and space your relative perspective on life reflects your relative position in life. (More speed)

At first, I suspect, what we discover in life may happen at random, then maybe by trail and error, and eventually, hopefully by more consistent forms and means of reason and logic, i.e., more consistent forms and means of reason and logic, i.e., more consistent way of understanding "reality". (Hold!)

The goal of learning – if I may become subjective for a moment and I say learning has a "goal" or a reason for taking place if learning has a goal, it is to understand, not knowledge for its own sake, or in its own abstraction, but to understand the nature (culture) of one's own reality, and how that reality connects with the rest of the universe.

(By now, part of the audience is intently listening while the other part is "bored".) (Faster.)

The basis of learning is – if I may now become an objective scientist – the simultaneity of thought and activity, i.e. we move about and we think. We think about out (Movement) activity and if we are conscious, we act on our thinking: Thought as an activity operates at the some time as the activity that stimulates thought – and I might add, all of the activity that goes on regardless of thought, out thought, that is. I don't want to show disrespect to those who believe in a supreme.

(Very fast delivery)

To continue, the effect of this simultaneity is to combine thought with the "material world", and to give reason to itself. Language allows us to explain thought and activity in the form of subject and object, person and other, being and becoming, as separate activities, separate processes.

Thus, we are able to consciously divide reality into many constituent parts by thinking of "it" that way. Our language is based on sound and speech, tomorrow's language will be based on the intellectual capacity of our artificial intelligence, the "computer". You see, to speak to a computer does not require sound or speech. So the language can and will evolve differently. (Pause)

(Now, slow delivery again)

PROF. TORTS

But right now, language allows us to communicate how we reflect upon our thoughts of the material world in terms of what that world means to us.

This is how – I suppose! - our expressions become the basis of our "culture." Our expressions become our culture, our culture, our expressions. Our language and cultural expressions become our lives of distinction.

(At this point, the "bored" group can take it no longer. As a matter of fact, this action is considered long overdue.)

Our lives become positioned according to the value we attribute to our collective language and culture. Our culture.....

(Now, the audience speaks.) (Unison)

ONE SIDE

A language for you and a language for me, first class citizens we shall be.
A language for you, and a language for me, first class citizens we shall be.

(In unison, the other side of the audience is up.)

OTHER SIDE

We are not passive absorbents who sit idly by while our sponges are poured into. No! We are human beings. Intellectual beings! You can't stand there and act as though there are no atrocities committed under the name of discovery, observation, and culture: As you say, that is your constituted right.

AUDIENCE

Lied about!

PROF. TORTS:

Oh! I beg to differ, we do not consider it lying so much as we believed it to be true. Obviously the white man's Egypt looks nothing like....

AUDIENCE

.... That's mythology!

PROF. TORTS

Sure it is, but when the shoe is on the other foot it looks differently.

SMART ASS

Of course, no two worlds are the same; no two world views are the same, isn't that your point?

PROF. TORTS

Exactly! No two worlds, no two world views are the same. That is exactly my point. What are we to expect?

AUDIENCE

What do you mean?

SMART ASS

Yes, I'd like to hear that too, what do you mean, western scholars during the height of European invasion of Africa, Asia, and the Americas......?

BLOOD

.... Don't forget Australia.

SMART ASS

.... Right, Australians were no more knowledgeable of the world out side of their limited framework than were the peoples whose land they stole, is that your point?

AUDIENCE

Right! They simply had more firepower.

SMART ASS

Exactly, and a more efficient way of communicating. We say, we shall not absorb!

(Streams begins to chant.)

STREAMS

Be it for REAL or on a screen, we shall not absorb.
Be it for REAL or on a screen, we shall n ot absorb.
Be it for REAL .... (Fade out as Prof Torts speaks in response to the audience outcry.)

[Observing movement of Streams]

BYSTANDER

There they go back and forth. There they go back and forth.

{…Torts continues as though nothing has happened, but responding to the notion "we shall not absorb"]

PROF. TORTS

That may not be such a bad idea: That is, to sit and absorb, for a change. Then maybe we can get you hot-heads to think rationally for a change. We understand that frustration may act as a catalyst for aggressive creativity, but it may also lead to self-defeat. You know, where you are consumed by your own energy: The energy of your own creation; spontaneous internal combustion. The Human Torch! Like the Phoenix?

SMART ASS

Like Richard Pryor!

(Explaining why Richard Pryor was chosen.)

That's more real, less metaphorical, to me. It's less steeped in the mythology debate. Also, that example fits into the category of verifiable events western science finds so necessary.

AUDIENCE

You will admit that western social scientists have had difficulty relating Egypt to Africa though, wont you? And, to the African-American? Isn't the Phoenix Pryor connection contrary to the Africa western historians have constructed?

SMART ASS

Your mean, painted!

AUDIENCE

Lied about!

PROF. TORTS

Oh! I beg to differ, we do not consider it lying so much as we believed it to be true. Obviously the white man's Egypt looks nothing like…..

AUDIENCE

……… That's mythology!

PROF. TORTS

Sure it is, but when the shoe is on the other foot it looks differently.

SMART ASS

Of course, no two world's are the same; no two world views are the same, isn't that your point?

PROF. TORTS

Exactly! No two worlds, no two world views are the same. That is exactly my point. What are we to expect?

AUDIENCE

What do you mean?

SMART ASS

Yes, I'd like to hear that too, what do you mean, western scholars during the height of European invasion of Africa, Asia, and the Americas......?

BLOOD

.... Don't forget Australia.

SMART ASS

...... Right, Australians were no more knowledgeable of the world out side of their limited framework than were the peoples whose land they stole, is that your point?

AUDIENCE

Right! They simply had more firepower.

SMART ASS

Exactly, and a more efficient way of communicating.

AUDIENCE

Prof. Torts, would you say this was the beginning of artificial intelligence?

PROF. TORTS

Do you mean the printing press or the calculating machine?

BLOOD

Now that you mentioned them, obviously both.   I hadn't thought of it that way. "Them that way", sorry.

PROF. TORTS

Sure, automatic technology definitely may count that as its beginning; those two machines, if they continues development that began around the 15/16 centuries is your starting point.

(Now alluding to protest.)

Interesting that your frame of reference is so recent, being that you raised the question about the Phoenix and Africa's Egypt, I would have expected you to go much further back. However, I get your point.

(Taking the opportunity to address the Phoenix)

BLOOD

That's not quite how it happened, I mean, about the "spontaneous internal combustion" discussion we touched up on briefly. That's not how our birth rights were taken away.

(The audience is now shown two simultaneous versions of how "it" happened, one the colonized people's version, the other, the white man's version. This is done through total simultaneous imagery (TSI).)

PROF. TORTS

Or, signed away by treaty! Again, depending on whose version you accept as representing a more accurate picture of what happened.

(Note: Blood changes his language as he gets more comfortable.)

BLOOD

The thang is yawl always trying to get us to be "objective", or, willing to accept your version of what happened, ours simply gets lost in the process. We are simply lying?

PROF. TORTS

Why do you say that?

BLOOD

Because you write the books!

PROF. TORTS

If you mean we keep records, yes we do that, but that's so everyone will know what happened.

SMART ASS

We keep records, too. At least, we used to.

PROF. TORTS

Yes, but yours were not accurate.

SMART ASS

Why? Because we chose to keep our records orally? Is that suppose to be our fault? Our reason for being alienated from our Birth Rights? Is that our fault? Because you came and successfully uprooted us from our space, is that supposed to be our fault?

PROF. TORTS

The record is clear, you sold your land to the European settlers.

CARETAKER

How could we sell what was not ours to sell?

PROF. TORTS

That's not my problem, your ancestors knew what they were doing.

(Again, total simultaneous imagery (TSI): One depicting a native council agreeing to share common property in common with the European; the other depicting "a legal bill of sale transferring land from the "Indians" to the European settlers.")

SMART ASS

We suffer because you used words that had no meanings for. We suffer because what you provide us with has no meaning to us: That is the nature of our alienation under your rule.

(At this point a quit unassuming "Indian" speaks. Southwestern accent.)

CARETAKER

Exactly! We are permanently outlawed from what belongs to nature. We are nature's children. Take nature's children away from HER safekeeping, and nature will tremble this Earth in pain until those children are retuned to her. That is the word given to us by our ancestors. Our ancestors said that it was impossible for them to "give" or "sell" the Europeans any "property". They had no right by our spiritual custom to make such as sale or, "treaty", as Europeans call it.

It was not theirs to do, and they did not do it. We believe our ancestors. Therefore, nature's land was taken away from her caretakers. And, each generation that goes by without returning nature's land back to us, there will be greater and greater hardship as more and more of her earth is eaten away by the greed of western science and technology: MARK MY WORD!

CARETAKER
(Now he changes, emotion is shown.)

...................And what so we have to show for it? High death rates, no work, no money, no land to cultivate. We have the dubious distinction of being the most exploited and maltreated of all "minorities" in the United States: That includes the African-American, the most widely discussed "minority" in this great land of ours, and the Mexican-American our blood brothers and sisters.

(Now with great pride.)

We are nations within a nation. Nations within nations if we include Mexico and Canada and Central America, on down below. Yet we – us, the native people of the Americas – find it virtually impossible to receive justice in "the most Democratic of Republics."

We have tried to live apart from these nations that consume us, but how?

(By now, everyone is listening with great intent.)

My question to you sir, you are a great scholar of your people. Tell me, are we suppose to be the model proto-type of your new world arrangement? Are we the "Braves" in your Brave New World? Is how you treat us your representative ideal of tomorrow?

(With everyone focused on Caretaker's strong statement, the streams appear as the African Support Choir.)
(Done as a "pop" tune/late 50's R&B.)

STREAMS
Is this for real? Are you always so ready to kill? Kill? Kill? Even the land that you steal? Is this for real?

(Fade out) (Repeat)

(Prof. Torts loses his cool for a moment – recovers quickly.)

PROF. TORTS
I don't find these interruptions contributing to our discussion. As a matter of fact, I find them rather annoying.

(Streams appear, again   (To audience)

STREAMS
Is he for real? Does he not follow our appeal? (then looking at Prof. Torts) Are you for real? Is that the deal? Are you for real? (Fade out)

(Prof. Torts now trying to conceal his anger with reason)

PROF. TORTS
You see, all these outbursts do are cause confusion, you don't want the truth to be heard.

(Audience)

(Serious challenge by Torts – Audience responds in kind)

AUDIENCE

Is he for real? HA! HA! HA! HA!

(Sort of embarrassed, perturbed with Torts)

WHITE ACTIVIST {This is a position not color of one's skin}

Sir, are you listening to what they are telling you? Can you hear? I think their questions are clear? At least, to my ear. (Laughter)

Should I repeat them for you? I happened to write them down just in case doing the course of the dialogue you might forget.

(Streams appear in sound – to be heard not seen)

(Question is very serious)

STREAMS

Is there no shame:
You are to blame! (Firm with authority-- not loud)

(Torts responds in kind. He believes what he's saying)

PROF. TORTS

I have no blame.
I have no shame.
Equity is my claim.
No Blame! No shame!
I have no reason to be ashamed. We live in the greatest civilization of all times.   Look at our accomplishments in roughly two or three hundred years. No other nat…………

(Steams cut in.) (In National Anthem form)

STREAMS

………..nation that kills with pride, all of those who lived inside, will freedom ring?

Will freedom ring?
Will freedom ring?

(Audience gives a response to streams.)

AUDIENCE RESPONSE

Freedom – we want out freedom.
Freedom – give us our freedom.
Freedom – everybody wants freedom.

BLOOD

Sure, tell us anything homeboi. We know! The niggas – excuse us – injuns brought this on themselves. Sure, brother man, we know! HA! HA! Tell us anything, we don't know no better. HA! HA! HA! HA!

(Audience laughs, too) (People are laughing while shaking their heads in disbelief knowing exactly what Prof. Torts meant.)

(Laughter stops simultaneously. One straggler shows mood with his bold laughter.)

PROF. TORTS

Mr. Moderator, I've had enough of these insults. Please control your audience or I shall have no choice but to conclude that I can no longer add any useful ideas to this discussion. I might add, such disruptions are a violation of my constitutional rights to free speech, and everybody else's right to assemble here freely, unmolested.

(Caretaker speaks in total disbelief. Raises question.)

CARETAKER

Do my people have a right to assemble freely on the land of our ancestors? Can we speak freely about how our birth rights were stolen from us? Huh? Can we do that without being called communists? What about our rights as self-contained nations?

PROF. TORTS

(To Caretaker)

What is your point? Mr. Moderator I've about had it up to here. (To Moderator with the emotional interruptions) I know that you people (To audience are caretaker).

AUDIENCE

You people? You people?

(The way Black people say it.)

PROF. TORTS

Yes, you people have had a rough go at it. But, that's not my fault, and I refuse to assume total responsibility for what might have happened to you in the past. That's all in the past, the unspeakable past. We must learn to let bygones be bygones. You must learn to live in the future.

(Watch here! Slow build up to argument)

AUDIENCE

The future is now! The past is upon us.

(Ignoring comment from audience.)

PROF. TORTS

Now, much of what you say is opinion.

AUDIENCE

Opinion? Our alienation, simply an opinion?

PROF. TORTS

No! No! Your observations.

AUDIENCE

Our deprivation?

PROF. TORTS

No, there is no duplication!

AUDIENCE

And, degradation?

PROF. TORTS

There's no verification of that.

AUDIENCE

You won't deny our subjugation!

PROF. TORTS

No, that's alienation!

AUDIENCE

Is that your observation?

PROF. TORT

You mean, your deprivation?

AUDIENCE

I mean you subjugation! (of us)

PROF. TORTS

There's no verification of your subjugation; no observation of any discrimination, no denial of your being, although your character may be questioned.

We are the future. There is no denial here. No distinctions are made here. We are one. There are no distinctions, here!

(Poet moves toward center stage repeating)

STREAMS

There are no distinctions; HERE!

Can't you see? There's us and we! And, we are free – or, (Pause) is there a fee?

(Leave stage; streams – poet speaks as a continuation to the thought)

POET SAID

No thoughts, anyway.
So, why do I tremble?
 Search? Wonder? Stumble?
Why can't I hear no dreams, anymore.
So, whom do I trouble?
Frighten? Threaten?

126

Whom do I threaten?

(Change)

(Response)

I think we have begun to listen! I think we have begun to hear!

(Questioning) Did you detect a slight contradiction, there? Yes, I would agree, but that is the nature of things here and now. Our new Politics of Culture.

We are ready to accept your observations Prof. Torts. No distinctions! Right now! Good! The Presidency! That's our first request!

(Looking of Prof. Torts saying, "I did not intend for it to be interpreted that way.")

(Poet rises again)

POET SAID
So whom do I trouble? Why do I tremble? Where do I wonder? Toward Pluto this time? Into a troubled world with a love of peace?

Will it be in this world? Or, the next? Our Love of Peace? And where are my dreams, anymore? Apparently, things are very satisfying, more and more! We live much better, now.

(Streams come and whisper to poet:)

They have invaded ANGOLA!

They have invaded GRENADA!

(Cry) Nicaragua, Mozambique, Wounded knee, Panama, Haiti, Dominican Republic, Somalia and Bosnia. (As though nothing was whispered.)

(Feeling proud)

POET SAID
I live much better, now that there are no distinctions.

(With astonishment)

But, why are they crying? (Change – serious)

Tell me, why are there acts of rebellion in Central America so often? Why, all-the-time? And in Africa, too? Obviously, the counterbalance to our American Democracy is the oppression of her other Americas. The other Americas.

Oh! I know! You're living yours! Your heaven is not located in the beyond, in the hereafter! No! Your heaven is right here on earth. It's right, here. SEE! SEE! (With deep anger) SEE!

(Wonder) We kill a thirty-six year old Grenadian simply because he was so kind as to (Crying – can't finish) .... as to (Really trying to comprehend.) How do we blow up a scholar like Walter Rodney? Please, explain? I don't understand! You say he was a communist?

Then, what about J. A. Rogers? We wouldn't publish his books. Why? And what happened to Albert Ayler? HA! HA! And, who is Albert Ayler? Huh? I bet you don't even know. I ought to embarrass, you (Looking right into the audiences' faces as one). Yea, that's right. I'd embarrass you over someone you ought to know.

Why should I allow you to allow our greatest creative gifts to remain anonymous, to us? HUH? NAW! NAW! (In street language) It ain't gone bees likes that!

I know you ain't never heard of Albert Ayler! I know! I know!

You don't know the names of who – let's see, who! - Let's say for the sake of argument – you don't know the names of three artists who died last year?

(With quick delivery)

Or, any of those people who were gunned down in your own community at the hands of a policeman's gun. Am I lying? I said, as I lying? I'm talking about ordinary people now.

(Baptist preacher, now)

You just name me one blood who you remember! Just one! One artist! One musician! Who made it past age 45.

(Back to poem)

No tear, all dry.

So, who keeps returning to the well?

Wishing? Crying? Confused?

(Now assuming the character of citizen)

Please Lord, let our leaders be telling the truth.

There must be meaning to our lives, Lord. Our adventures across the seas must be for peace, ARE THEY NOT, Lord. (Pause)

POET SAID

One simple question, why would our government destroy the New Jewel Movement papers? Excuse me, the Black Panther papers? And, what do you suppose happened to Adam's records? Who is Adam? Adam Clayton Powell! I know, there are so many, aren't there. But, Adam? You mean we can go almost anywhere we please now, and we don't even remember Adam? Phew! Now, that's heavy!

Anyway, let's go on. (Matter of factly) I've got you here so I might as well say what's on my mind. These occasion don't come that often. But the time has come, and if nobody but these walls hear what I speak, somebody's got to say it.

(Half humorously/half seriously)

Hell, I aint tryin to be no sacrificial lamb! I don't taste like lamb, anyway. That I am certain of. You may run with that as you please. But, we can't let the legend of Adam & A. Phillip & Dubois & Robeson & Mary McCleod & Fannie Lou & Rosa Parks & our slain die, too. We can't do that! That's suicide! Did you hear me folks. I said that is genocide! Fratricide! Do you get my point! (Then lightens up!)

You know where I'm coming from! It's only natural that now's the time. Now is the time, there's no serious debate about that! WE MUST MOVE! AS ONE! AS ONE HUMANITY!

We have earned the right to PARTAKE IN, ALL offerings. All offerings. All of them! That includes the discussion around who has the right to declare us extinguishable. It's just that simple. It's just! That simple!

There is going to be an EARTH with people on it. People who look like you and me and us. The laws of distributive justice say that the social and the earth body must share equivalently, not in adverse proportions to individual and social wealth. WE WANT THIS EARTH KEPT ALIVE!

(The moderator approaches the podium for the first time, and interestingly, he appears confident.)

(Because what he is about to ask is so complex, yet so simple, it must be read or recited in a manner that allows everyone to – "get it" the first time. Now, it will be for a moment; and may people will ponder it further, that's O.K. It's difficult but let them feel the question. Feel it in essence.) (Listening)

MODERATOR
Mr. Speaker, Mr. Spencer-Brown, I believe a fellow countryman of yours has written in Laws of Form that "there can be no motive unless contents are seen to differ in value."

I suspect I lost most of you so I'll repeat again, Spencer-Brown said that "there can be no distinction without motive; and there can be no motive unless contents are seen to differ in value." You said, there are no distinctions, here. And, I take it you were limiting your comment to this room. So my question is, how would you define Birth Right as a first principle of culture.

PROF. TORTS
(Obviously, Prof. Torts was an excellent Barrister in Great Britain because, although the Moderator's question literally floored him, he recovered rather well.)

I'll be very honest, I was not prepared for today.

(Laughter)

But, let me try anyway. (Attention) I've never been so happy to have had legal training.

(Laughter. Referring to his background before becoming a "Philosopher of Artificial Intelligence" and how helpful it has been today, he goes right into……)

PROF. TORTS
What is rightfully yours at birth continues with you throughout life, unless that right is released to some else. (Hiss! Hiss! Hiss! Come from audience) For example, if you have the talent…….. (He should always be heard clearly, not matter what) Let's say you have the ability to compose music lyrics and the score, I believe they call it. That's your talent, yours skill. And let's say that you wrote a beautiful ballad that you were sure would become a hit. However, there's a problem. No one will offer you a contract. Let's say further that you are accomplished as a musician. Here's the deal! A recording company representative stopped by the local Five Spot and heard your group perform. He offered you a deal right there on the spot: The deal was how would you like to record for International Jazz? They – meaning International Jazz – would produce, etc, your album. You would record your music, with your group or with your selection of musicians. Whatever!

(Actor-Jazz musician appears)

JAZZ MAN

Oh, shit! Is this for real? Did you hear that, I-we-got a recording contract. We can make our record. Record our own music.

PROF. TORTS

You make your record. Record you music.small hit. In other words, you make it big as a jazz musician.

While listening to the radio one day someone very famous hears you LP and likes a particular tune: The Ballad! He calls up his manager, etc., etc.,

(Stop! Better Example)

They get your name, call you up and say….. No, let's make the even more direct. You are sitting, listening to the radio one day and your tune - The Ballad! - comes on sung by the famous pop star. You say, ………

JAZZ MAN

…..Oh! Shit! That's my song: That's my music "pop star" is singing there. Oh, shit! I'm going to be rich! And, famous, too.

PROF. TORTS

What you did not know was when you signed that recording contract, the only thing you were allowed to do was record your music. You didn't own the rights to "nothing". Not even your own music, recorded by you. Nothing!

Oh sure you become famous. People see you and say, "you're the one who wrote that beautiful ballad. Give me your autograph." Can you tell them, Jazz man?

JAZZ MAN

Yes, I wrote it, but it ain't mine! I don't own it. I released my rights to that tune when I cut my first album. Ain't that some shit!

NARRATOR

(The audience was stunned, This argument presented so well by Prof. Torts and verified by his witness to the facts, and all. As I said, Prof. Torts recovered from the question rather well. So the audience sat telling each other stories of a dude who don't get no royalties, and that 's his tune. He wrote it! His name is on it, but he can't collect a dime.)

(Then out of frustration.)

AUDIENCE

Prof. Torts what you say we know all too well, but that ain't the half of it. I can tell you……….

(Blood to the rescue.)

(Mingus composition plays as intro and throughout.)

AFRICAN CHOIR--WITH BLOOD

…… Mingus was Dead! Mingus was dead! Mingus was dead long before we recognized his genius.

BLOOD

Charles Mingus had to die before we knew that he had even lived. Such strange words from a people who created Mingus. Such irony of being!

CHOIR

(Sing) Such is the nature of becoming. Such is the nature of recognition.

BLOOD

Such a strange way for a people who have suffered so greatly, so long......

CHOIR

(Sing) Such is the nature of restriction/oppression. Such is the nature of non-recognition, to never know, to overlook such a creative genius. Mingus the Genius. Mingus the Genius. The Genius of Mingus. Mingus the Genius. Mingus the Genius. The Genius of Mingus.

BLOOD

But, we never recognized his genius, his creativity while he lived. It's like we are determined to follow the dictates of others in spite of our intuitive inclination.

SMART ASS

Is this the proper way we should act? Playing the roles others have drawn out for us?

CHOIR

Yet, no respect is forth coming.

BLOOD

Still we do not know how much our ancestors gave to humanity.

(Becomes a Mingus Hymn, here)

CHOIR

Mingus had to die before we discovered he had ever been her with us. The Pathos of Americanism has caused us to disbelieve the value of our being. So Mingus/Hughes died and we sill do not know who they are. Their creativity unsurpassed and but we are told it's Styron/Faulkner whom we should love: failing to remind us that we heard more about Faulkner and Styron in the sixties than we did about Wright/ Ellington/Davis/ Ossie Dee combined.

(Start Rock n Rhythm and Mingus hymn clash, then become one.) (Repeat)

It was "Amos & Andy" updated we see each week. Never once did Coltrane have us view him live in color on ABCBNBC Coltrane was a casualty of the war in Vietnam, all of it in living/dead color on the ABCBNBC.

(Rock n Rhythm sung as a counter point is Mingus composition and lyrics.)

Rock n Rhythm Rock n Rhythm Rock n Rhythm Rock n Rhythm

BLOOD

Ornette Coleman and Don Cherry had no meals for their art.

CHOIR

But we supported Black art in the sixties/ seventies. Rock n Rhythm.

BLOOD

Yes, for 2 years, 3 months, 5 days, 11 hours, 8 seconds, 0.001. It was Faulkner-Styron's history that we learned.

CHOIR

But how were we to know? We ain't never had no history before. Rock n Rhythm.

BLOOD:

Before Styron created Nat Turner.

CHOIR

Didn't we say, Mingus is dead! Didn't we, Mingus is Dead! Who? Charles Mingus. Rock n rhythm.

BLOOD

He dead, you know while we listened to the latest craze: Syn-the-tic Articificial Music.

CHIOR

What is Syn-the-tic Ar-ti-fi-cial Music? Rock n Rhythm (repeat)

BLOOD

Synthetic Artificial Music is artificially created/copied, electronically reproduced sound designed to simulate musical forms created/produced by beings of consciousness.

CHOIR

A copy of musical forms reproduced to sound like the music it intends to represent. Rock n Rhythm.

BLOOD

What do they call it? Do they call it the Gospel?

CHOIR

No! Rock n Rhythm (Repeat)

BLOOD

Do they call it, Blues?

CHOIR

No! Rock n Rhythm, Rock n Rhythm, Rock n Rhythm, Rock n Rhythm.

BLOOD

Do they call, Jazz? Rock n Rhythm, Rock n Rhythm

CHOIR

What's Jazz? No! Rock n Rhythm, Rock n Rhythm

BLOOD

Do they call it the Rhythm and Blues? Rock n Rhythm, Rock n Rhythm.

CHOIR

No! No! Rock n Rhythm. (Repeat)

BLOOD

Do they call it Country & Western? Rock n Rhythm.

CHOIR

Country & Western? Country & Western? Rock n Rhythm.

BLOOD

Do they call it Hill Billy? Rock n Rhythm.

CHOIR

Hill Billy, you mean Blue Grass? No! Rock n Rhythm.

BLOOD

Do they call it Rock & Roll? HUH? Rock n Rhythm.

CHOIR

Rock n Roll? Rock n Roll? Rock n Roll? Rock n Roll? No! Rock n Rhythm, Rock n Rhythm.

BLOOD

Do they call it Soul! Does it have Soul?

CHOIR

Rock n Roll?

BLOOD

No!

CHOIR

Blue Grass?

BLOOD

No!

CHOIR

Country & Western?

BLOOD

No!

CHOIR

Rhythm & Blues?

BLOOD

No!

CHOIR

Jazz?

BLOOD

Jazz? What's Jazz? No?

CHOIR

The Blues?

BLOOD

No!

CHOIR

The Gospel?

BLOOD

No!

CHOIR:

Then what do they call it? The Syn-the-tic Artifi-cial Music? What do they call it? SAM? SAM? Rock n Rhythm.

BLOOD

SAM? Not a bad idea! SAM! No, not SAM, DISCO! It's called Disco, Disturbing Interstitial Sounds Causes Depression.

CHOIR

Rock n Rhythm, Rock n Rhythm.

(Exit to applauds from audience)

Disco means Syn-the-tic Artificial Music: Disco SAM, Disco DAM, Rock n Rhythm, Rock n Rhythm, Disco SAM, Rock n Rhythm, Disco Sam, Rock n Rhythm, (Repeat)

(Audience is wondering what /who next? Whoo-we!)

CARETAKER

I find your question – Mr. Moderator – very timely. And for that, in the name of our ancestor and the creator we thank you.

And, you, Prof. Torts, your legal reasoning is obviously of superior quality. You are well grounded in the logic of western civilization.

Blood, I always knew you were talented, but I never would have thought to give that kind of response. Brilliant! And the chorus…. (Shaking Head, "unbelievable")

Anyway, while listening I had plenty of time to meditate. Coming out of meditation, it was revealed to me that although Prof. Torts was well versed in the philosophy of private property: and Blood in the logic of oppression, that is not our way.

Neither represented a response I could be satisfied in giving. No, that is not how I should respond to the question regarding birth rights, culture, and distinction. You see, in our document, The Hau De No Sau Nee, a Basic Call to Consciousness: Address to the Western World, Geneva, Switzerland, autumn, 1977, states that the The Hau De No Sau Nee have no concept of private property…….

"Before the colonists came, we had no consciousness about a concept of commodities. Everything, even the things we make belong to the creators of life and are to be returned ceremonially, an in reality, to the owners. Our people live a simple life, one unencumbered by the need of endless material commodities. The fact is that their needs are easily met. It is also true that our means of distribution is an eminently fair process, one in which all of the people share in all the material wealth all of the time……"

" Ours was a wealthy society. No one suffered from want. All had the right to food, clothing, and shelter. All shared in the bounty of the spiritual ceremonies and the natural work no one stood in any material relationship of power over anyone else. No one could deny anyone access to the things they needed. All in all, before the colonists came, ours was a beautiful and rewarding way of life." So, for us, the native people of North America, the idea of birth right is synonymous with the Creator. One cannot exist without the other.

NARRATOR
(Obviously, no one came to the forum expecting to be a party to this encounter. I wonder if anyone brought a tape recorder?)

CARETAKER
That brings me to a rather strange document our ancestors have passed on from the time they discovered it. As the story is told, the Six Nations Iroquois Confederacy "scout" in reality a Hau de no sau nee team – was visiting some outposts of the Confederacy when a very unusual object was found. (As Caretaker pulls out the "unusual object", the audience looks, but with no great deal of attention or concern.)

I'd like to play this objects voice recorder, and let hear what my ancestors heard after they discovered it.

SMART ASS
When did they discover it? (With a sort of laughter in his voice.)

AUDIENCE:
HA! HA! HA!

CARETAKER
In sixteen twenty eight, your recorded time.

(Upon examining the document…..)

SMART ASS

Wait a minute. That's a late model tape recorder, from here it looks to be around 1984 when it came out. How can that be a tape recorder found 1628 when tape recorders were not made until the twentieth century. What kind of game you trying to run, brother man?

CARETAKER:

Hold on! You Americans must learn how too listen. You are too ready to shoot from the jump, as you put it. The inscription reads right on the label, made in South Africa, 1984, A.D., Polaroid.

SMART ASS

("You mean from the hip! (jump? HA!) ")

AUDIENCE

HA! HA! HA! HA! Polaroid makes cameras! You know, like the ones that take pictures of our African brothers and sisters in South Africa. The ones they carry with their pass-ports. Man you way off. That's today! I don't know what's on it, but you just picked that up recently. Now, you/it may have some heavy things to say, but why the trickery?

CARETAKER

Look at it yourselves? (Beyond their wildest imagination.) (As we watch the image, a woman is speaking.)

AZANIA

They destroyed nature's calendar.... Why am I treated so bad? Tell me! Is this the nature of people from western civilization? They destroyed nature's calendar.

(Now from 3rd person to 1st and 2nd.)

You have given me your name and number, a "passbook", you call it. Yet, I live like a refugee at home. At home, I'm treated like an alien. At home, I'm alienated. At Home!

(Caretaker interjects comment while someone makes an inaudible statement.)

CARETAKER

Someone said, "What's western civilization?", right in the middle of her statement. We never figured out how that got on the tape. (Tape: rewinds)

UNKNOWN VOICE:

........At Home! What's western civilization?

URBAN CHORUS

Take it to the streets, take it to the streets.

(Images are now of whatever is mentioned.)

Rock n Rhythm (Repeat)

AZANIA

I'm human! I have distinguishable features – if that's important to you – a face, feelings, desires, a culture, a collective will: We are universal! No need to say, too. Desires are universal. Greed is vengeful. Nature's desire is universal. Man's desire is universal. Man's selfishness is self annihilation.

STREAMS

Take it to the streets. Take it to the streets.

U.C.

Rock n Rhythm. (Repeat)

UNKNOWN VOICE

What is western civilization?

AZANIA

Does nature desire that human's extermination be fulfilled? Is that nature's desire? I wonder what argument provides the best logic for self annihilation? Is it a sense of denial or a desire for recognition that has thrown us out of balance?

STREAMS

Tell us a lie
Do or dieROCK
Say bye, byeN(REPEAT)
Why should we tryRHYTHM
That's why our cry

AZANIA

Red or blue?   What is the difference?

STREAMS

The Dreams Alive. Dreams never die. Rock n Rhythm, Rock n Rhythm.

AZANIA

A cry in the night the end is com..........

STREAMS

A cry in the night
The end is in sight
A perfect laser flight
But dreams never die
Their beginning is in the eye.
Rock n Rhythm, Rock n Rhythm

AZANIA

But tell me, what is our love? Love of peace?
Love of dream? Love of life? Love of desire?
Desire death? Do we desire death?

STREAMS

The dreams alive, long live the dreams.
AAAAH!   AAAAH!
The dream's alive, dreams never......
Rock n Rhythm

AZANIA

Believe? Is heaven beyond our dreams realized? Are we there, yet? Are we there? So soon? By whose judgement?

STREAMS

Is that it?(Rock n Rhythm)
Is it there?(Rock n Rhythm)
Is it there?(Rock n Rhythm)

AZANIA

Outlaws! Space Bandits! 1984, Par Excellence.
Star Wars Forever, Kimberley Mines, Citicorp, GM, ITT, IBM, ICBM, USA, SCBM, USSR, BMENS, USA, - Union of South Africa! Red or Blue?
What's the difference when the life ending forces threaten to deny the human will/ recognition as living, breathing intellectual beings?
Well, what's the difference? I've put a question ON THE FLOOR.
Have we been consuming too much? Intellectual beings, has there been too much food for thought?
Greed! Is it greed? Insecurity about never having enough? Well, is that it?

UNKNOWN VOICE

What is western civilization?

(Although speaker in the video letter cannot hear the other questioner, she appears to raise her question right on time.)

AZANIA

I don't know, would pride drive such a hard bargain. Whereby red or blue really makes no difference in pride and greed, are they opposites?

Is that why I'm treated so bad? Is that the key?
Do the absurd simply to keep "our" competition from doing it first? Is that the key?

UNKNOWN VOICE

What is western civilization?

STREAMS

Perrier is Mother Earth's first soft drink. Drink soft drink.

U.C.

drink soft drink. Rock n Rhythm.

AZANIA

Tarzan is dead! Yet (Pause) amazingly Africa (Pause) we (Pause) are alive. It is at great expense. The suffering and pain of my people have become unbearable! Heavy suffering! Great pain! The death, theft, and a rape are beyond imagination. Our imagination! So, I know you're not surprised we're not doing too well.

(Understated)

Twenty four countries are facing starvation, and this use to be a land-o-plenty. The western countries act like everything's okay.

URBAN CHORUS

Everything's okay.(Rock n Rhythm)
Don't you say.(Rock n Rhythm)
Everything's okay.(Rock n Rhythm)
We have our way.(Rock n Rhythm)
Everything's okay.(Rock n Rhythm)

AZANIA

Tarzan is dead! Cowboys run America. I know its not forever, but how does it feel to be free? Two countries with enough weapons to destroy forever, for us. And, now I understand that my oppressors have one, too. They say life couldn't have been better, for us.

(Pause)

By the way, did I say those countries are in Africa, the ones starving? No home grown food! You get the drift? No home grown food. None. STARVATION!

But, what can we do? Our land is all through? Can we do for ourselves? Can we do what others avoid so easily while they tell us "violence is not the way to freedom? While death squads go about killing at will." Whom so they kill? Subversives!

URBAN CHORUS

Take it to the street! Why should you care? Take it to the streets! You are not there. (Rock n Rhythm)

AZANIA

Why should you care? Why should you? Can you say, without giving it a second thought, I want to free humankind from our oppressive tendencies whatever they may be? I want to further human understanding.

What ever else we do in life, I want to add value to or enlightenment. Can you say that without a second thought? Without looking over your shoulder, so the speak?

(Pause)

Is a nuclear bomb going to further human understanding? Will this be our unique contribution to nature's movement? Can't we wait for the sun? It may die in time. (Change) The future is under our care only when we learn what has meaning: learn that truth may be, but when it has no meaning to those expected of believe it, that truth is unto itself an abstraction. (Pause) But that's not the least of our problems, since our understanding of events can differ so greatly when you see my account of what happened, you should be aware that it may differ as greatly from any other account as March differs from December. Whatever!

Remember, my reflections of what happened are the reflections of what happened are the reflections of the victim: Theirs, the conqueror.......

.......since our understanding of events will/can differ so greatly, our dilemma is how to act correctly.

UNKNOWN VOICE

What's western civilization?

STREAMS

Take it to the street! First strike ability. Take it to the street. You got mobility. (Rock n Rhythm, Rock n Rhythm, Rock n Rhythm, Rock n Rhythm)

AZANIA:Our dilemma? Un/re/doing ourselves. That's HARD! Death is easy. It's living that is causing us so much strife, Pain.......

It's inevitable! Why not end the process – living by exploding the final solution to every living soul, and see where that event will place us in space – time.

Why not?

I DEFY NATURE! Say it, I DEFY NATURE! Our beginning seems a good one.

Look, when it's normal for urban dwellers to expect people in rural countries to feed us and starve themselves, redoing the self is hard. VERY HARD!

Can you imagine if we were boycotted by the producers of food? All of us?

What a contradiction? So, why not? Why not end it all now? As an anti-life argument, it seems logical, does it not?

Tarzan is Dead! And, the Redskins are in the Super Bowl, again. Beaten! Same people! "Savages!" By the way, where are the Red people who once were the caretakers of this land named in honor of liberty?

NARRATOR

(God Bless America)

UNKNOWN VOICE

[It's their dream that kept us alive. What's a Redskin?)

STREAMS

The Dream's Alive!

The Dream's Alive!

Rock n Rhythm, Rock n Rhythm, Rock n Rhythm, Rock n Rhythm, Rock n Rhythm, Rock n Rhythm.

AZANIA

If the eternal flame is our claim, if the sun has cooked your brain, excuse me, if the sun is our worship, can we not learn a very simple lesson from those who long ago converted conflagration into a ritual of the "Sun God"? Such a simple lesson! Native people of the western hemisphere, do you think you can teach them the dance so you don't have to go through this trauma of the new world civilization?

STREAMS

This ain't no jive.

URBAN CHORUS

The Dream's Alive
When The Clock Strikes Five
Give yourself a Treat
Dance to the Beat.
Dance to the Beat.
Rock n Rhythm, Rock n Rhythm, Rock n Rhythm, Rock n Rhythm, Rock n Rhythm, Rock n Rhythm.

UNKNOWN VOICE

What's a Redskin?
Where's The New World?
What's Western Civilization?
(The audience is now dumbfounded. Is this......)

PROF. TORT

Folly! Pure Folly!
(The audience response is quick.)

BLOOD:

NO! Wait! The speaker here was excellent! She started me to thinking, so I forget I was here. But I was referring to how they told us things would be better for us. All we had to do was adopt the ways of the new world.

CARETAKER

For them, it was nothing. For us, we gave up everything. I guess it seemed so easy because our culture was integrated. Everything interacted. They simple divided...... Yes, I know exactly what you mean. Everything related to nature's process of growth and development. We weren't competing with anyone or anything. Nature's environment was not an enemy we had to compete with; anything we had to subdue. Conquer! Destroy! Do you know the American has wasted more of nature's resources than.....?

STREAMS

.......The law allows, if I may interject. The problem is, some of us – those in control, let's say for the moment – do not agree with those communistic notions.

CARETAKER:

Communistic is to live in harmony? And, we should oppose that/ To live in harmony with nature – as intellectual beings ought to be capable of - is the sin? Is that the sin? A U.S. Secretary of Interior said that the "American Indians failed/ died because they practiced socialism." Is that our sin? Oh! No! I don't believe that! If that's the sin? Where do we begin? If that's the sin, were does life begin?

STREAMS

Look, we have more people living at the highest standard.

UNKNOWN VOICE

Possible. More than at any other time.

CARETAKER

I maintain that your statement is incorrect. We had the highest standard of living. We consciously did not need technology to find our spirituality. We followed nature's signals, her patterns, her movements. Everything had a balance.

ARLENE

Where humans given the responsibility of completing this phase of nature's movement?

MODERATOR

You mean "were"?

ARLENE

I said "were," What did I say?

BLOOD

I said, "where".

PROF. TORTS

I'm not sure I understand your question.

MODERATOR

I think she means………

ARLENE

I am capable of saying what I mean.

MODERATOR

I was only………..

ARLENE

And, I appreciate that. But, I am capable of explaining what I mean. My question is simply this. What if the universe is so constructed that along the way something is always set in motion to trigger another process? You know like the going and coming of events? And, what if we are that process?

PROF. TORTS

Pre-destiny!

ARLENE

Are we predestined to make earth uninhabitable? Is that our role? Should we allow them to continue making bombs? Why should I bother to work? You're gonna blow the whole place up anyway.

BLOOD

Right on sister!

PROF. TORTS

Obviously I cannot answer all of those questions – you were talking to me, weren't you. All of you…….

ARLENE

……..It's directed toward everything…….

142

PROF. TORTS

.......seen to have chosen me as tonight's target. So I'll respond to the best of my ability. The world is just not that simple anymore, if it ever were.

ARLENE

So what is the meaning of Birth Right? That seems to be why we're here anyway. Some of us, that is.

BLOOD

It means that all of us have a right to the value of our product. Human labor is required of us – even when the labor results in the creation of artificial intelligence – as intellectual beings, our minds and bodies function best when we are active. Nature gave us the space, ingredients, and ability to construct our own realities, erect our own restrictions, manifest our own dreams, annihilate our own selves. That's our right from birth.

PROF. TORTS

You believe in free will!

BLOOD

I believe we were given the things ABOVE. How we construct, use, apply, destroy is our business. Our contradiction. The urge in Western man – the American leadership- is to test nature; disrupt it completely and totally to see what will happen to humankind. I can go it alone!

ARLENE

That seems kind of crazy to me.

BLOOD

Death Wish!

STREAMS

Death wish. Death wish. Death wish. Death wish.

URBAN CHORUS

(Repeat while other half on loud speaker speaks.)
Better Dead than Red
Better Lead than Bread
Better Said than Dread

(Repeat)

PROF. TORTS

I say folly to you, you old boy. The modern world, or, the west, if you will, only wants to exploit nature's resources to help us realize our potential. That's what it's there for. Our use. We are not the only beings nature created to use tools, but logical progression says that the more we learn, the more we know. The more we know, the more complex our systems become the more materials we need.

CARETAKER

Technology! You left out technology.

PROF. TORTS

I see no need to mention it because this is not what we are arguing about. Birth right, and before that learning were the basis of our discussion. I was not aware that it had become a discussion on technology. I said materials.

ARLENE

How can you talk about birth right and not discuss technology? Didn't the white man use the gun as his most effective invention for acquiring land? Is that not correct? Is that technology?

PROF. TORTS

That might be true, but we want to live, too. We are not interested in destroy......

(At that point Poet Said Saud begins.......)

PROF. TORTS

.....I said materials!

POET SAID

....I use to meditate (is how Poet Said begins. Then he follows with) Now, I just sit and stare at reality.

UNKNOWN VOICE

(There it went!)

POET SAID

I use to search for meaning. Now, I just walk around aimlessly.

(Unknown Voice: Where am I?) I use to cry out, give me liberty, I want to let I be, all of us are equal and free. Turn off that learning tree.

STREAMS

(Unknown Voice: What happened?) Now, I just say, give me a cup of tea, I want to sit on your knee, all of us are alien to thee, TURN ON THAT LEARNING TREE, WHY ARE WE ALIEN TO THEE?

WHY ARE WE ALIEN TO WE?

(Arlene is transformed into Mother Earth as she begins to speak, but only after she has been "moved" during the reading of Poet Said.)

POET SAID

I wasn't going to comment except by way of question, but after giving it some thought, I've decided to speak my peace. It's been some time, now, since I've had a forum from which to speak.

Since man, and I say man specifically – assumed direct responsibility and claimed direct dependency from the Creator, he also claimed to be the original recipient of "God's work." As the original recipient of God's word, man's responsibility thus became – that of caretaker of this Earth. As caretaker, man thereby given power of attorney status and all of the rights and privileges invested in such status.

Man, under this arrangement, obviously could claim not only direct dependency and responsibility, but also the original position itself, by way of power of attorney. As surrogate, man assumed it was his role to speak for and to God. Man therefore becomes God's spokesman, interpreter, executor, and confidante. What an enormous responsibility invested in one fraction – minute fraction – minute fraction – of "God's" creations. Man alone was given the responsibility to govern this earth. Only man could decide how much when. He could even decide what.

But what was to be the "checks and balance"? Who was to maintain the equilibrium? Regulate the ecology? Advise man?

God! Yes, no one else but God. Only God could speak to man from a position of authority. Only man could talk to God.

Somehow in building this equation, man seems to have created a myth: AN ILLUSION of a lost imagination, if you will.

Whether one relies on logic or truth, the question must be the same, did the creator give man complete self retaliating power over this Earth? Or, was the evolution of intellectual beings simply an occurrence that neither signaled man's superior status or unique relationship to "God"?

(Streams appear dressed in white.)

STREAMS
Abuse Mother Earth,
Destroy Nature's Life.
Abuse our land,
Destroy nature's breath.
Abuse the spirit,
Destroy life's soul.
Abuse yourself,
And, now is forever.
Why not, end now forever?
Now is forever
End all forever (repeat last two lines)
(Streams disappear, Mother Earth returns.)

MOTHER EARTH
It may very well be true that man's universe is billions of years old – a highly understated proposition – but does that give man the right to conclude human life within its infancy?

Who gave man that right? His own intellect? Man simply thought of it all by himself? (Observation)

Power of attorney status – even if it were given to man alone – and, I repeat MAN ALONE – does not grant man the right to destroy his own life, other forms of existence.

Let's be real, would the all knowing creator place all, or some creations under the jurisdiction of a self destructive infant? Under a boogooloo wobbeling set of beings, who when they are told by me to stop – continue their destructive path? Am I, Mother Earth, to end up like all of the other parts of man's universe? Destroyed! Lifeless! Barren!

Look, all around you. Look! Lifeless! Barren!

No one there!

STREAMS

White Boi, White Boi, Where are you coming from?
White Boi, White Boi, Where are we goin?
White Boi, White Boi, Where are you come in from?
Where do we belong?

Is this earth not kind enough! A kind enough place? To house every living thing that come from/to Mother Earth's space.

MOTHER EARTH

Do you realize how much time – space it took to build an equation that would allow life to evolve in its many manifestations? All in one setting? There was no "survival of the fittest," here. Everything had a checks and balance, rhythm, harmony, form, time, space, movement.

Do you understand what it took to create such a balance: one, and many evolving constituents? Complimenting each others rhythm? Simultaneously? Look, what it amounts to is this, since the advent of western civilization, you have destroyed life's forces not one by one, but in droves and droves, in perpetuity; beyond anything measureable by the manual of creation. Is it greed? I don't know, but it's coming down to something's gotta give, you know what I mean? I've sat back and observed you human life, or other forms of existence.

Let's be real, would the all knowing creator place all, or some creations under the jurisdiction of a self destructive infant? Under a boogooloo wobbeling set of beings, who when they are told by me to stop – continue their destructive path? Am I, Mother Earth, to end up like all of the other parts of man's universe? Destroyed! Lifeless! Barren!

Look, all around you. Look! Lifeless! Barren! No one there!

STREAMS

White Boi, White Boi, Where are you coming from?
White Boi, White Boi, Where are we goin?
White Boi, White Boi, Where are you come in from?
Where do we belong?
Is this Earth not kind enough! A kind enough place? To house every living thing that come from/to Mother Earth's space.

MOTHER EARTH

Do you realize how much time – space it took to build an equation that would allow life to evolve in its many manifestations? All in one setting? There was no "survival of the fittest," here. Everything had a checks and balance, rhythm, harmony, form, time, space, movement.

Do you understand what it took to create such a balance: one, and many evolving constituents? Complimenting each others rhythm? Simultaneously? Look, what it amounts to is this, since the advent of western civilization, you have destroyed life's forces not one by one, but in droves and droves, in perpetuity; beyond anything measurable by the manual of creation. Is it greed? I don't know, but it's coming down to something's gotta give, you know what I mean? I've sat back and observed you destroy – no kill – thousands upon thousands of life's species: Birds, plants, people, bison, you name it. You didn't care. If it served your purpose........

STREAMS

..........If it serves your purposes, you know what to do, kill it. If it serves your purpose, you know what to do, take it.

If it serves your purpose, you know what to do, experiment with it. If it serves your purpose, you know what to do, you know what to do!

MOTHER EARTH

If it, (Pause) if it were not me – I can be selfish, too – you are abusing and destroying, some of the things you have done are simply unbelievable. Simply unbelievable! For instance, why would you destroy billions of square feet of timber and then turn around and build a park in memory of someone who has more often than not taken life, human, and/or otherwise.

Unbelievable!

You killed people who were already building a vast reservoir of nature's logic and rebuilding process. Then you had to build a Botanic Garden to relearn what you destroyed. How many in Europe alone! Two million? Is that overstated?

And, in the process, as your reward, you became the medical doctor, medicine man, health control agent. Brilliant! You are still searching for the secrets. Look, they are right here. Look all around you. Secrets!

STREAMS

But the bush is gone. So are the trees. The birds. Oh such beautiful birds. Where are my beautiful birds?

MOTHER EARTH

You do not make life, not yet. You only reproduce it. No matter the form you discover, it simply allows you to reproduce it many different ways.

But you haven't discovered the secret of making my beautiful birds. Want my birds back. And, I want my trees, my life……You know what I'm talking about.

You must remember all life is important to me. So what did you suppose that I graded life according to superior – inferior distinctions? I make no distinction between human life and other life forms. That's your illusion. That's your image creation. You were granted the mind to think.

My life is of and from me, and the sun of course. (All praise (s) to our sun and the moon.) Without me there is no you, for now.

So if you plan to move on, move on! Don't kill life here then run. Is that to be your contribution to "the universe"? Must you be so crude? So destructive?

Is, hell you calling? Remember your bombs? Interestingly, you have so many ways to kill this earth. So many! I bet you don't get a chance to discover all of them.

(Streams enter walk toward audience and say)

STREAMS

Wanna bet? Anybody wanna bet?

(Ad lib, Repeat only if necessary, i.e. to make the point, point much clearer.)

MOTHER EARTH

You see, that is the logic of the perfect lie. Keep lying (rationalizing), and you'll destroy yourselves before you find the antidote to death. Your greatest dream. Life! Your greatest nightmare, death! Now, wait-a-minute, I am not proposing apocalypse, you are.

(Speaking for Mother Earth)

STREAMS

I didn't make the bombs, you did. Are you for real? You mean there's no hope except through building more bombs? What logic – the perfect lie. Brilliant. Simply brilliant! Mad, but brilliant as D.Q. would say. Such logic. Anti-logic.

DOUBTY

Don't you think you are ex.........

MOTHER EARTH

......STOP!Don't even try it! Do you know now long the list is, don't even try it. Don't get me angry.

DON'T MAKE ME ANGRY. Up to now I've been rather patient. Too patient! Don't make me angry.

For those improprieties will be longer than the last ice age next time. You want to live in hell, I'll let you live in hell.

BLOOD

Another way to look at it is we've been here over three million years and three million years is three million years.

SMART ASS

Five million years. Man, where you been? Its five million years since the first homo-sapiens was discovered in Africa. And knowing the white man, I'd add another ten million years, and still think I'm too low.

FRANKIE

Now that's dumb! Mother Earth, or A.P. – whoever it is – just told Prof. Torts that his shit ain't gon work, how you think you can get away with some rank shit like that.

MOTHER EARTH

People! People! Just be quiet, and listen. O.K.?

DOUBTY

Well, you certainly don't have any faith in us do you?

MOTHER EARTH

On the contrary, it is because you have chosen such a dangerous path that I find it necessary to say these harsh things.

When I spoke with a non-threatening voice, you refused to hear me. Now you tell me I am being too harsh.

You never cease to amaze me. You always want it both ways. All the time. My, how selfish! I'll give it to you both ways.

DOUBTY

Yes, but how can we get ahead when you say all of these negative things about us.

(After hearing the complete discourse, Prof. Torts now offers)

PROF. TORTS

We need new explanations.

DOUBTY

What was that?

PROF. TORTS

We need new explanations about the new technology, and how it affects the dynamics of our emerging world. Our old answers simply will not work in tomorrow's new world.

DOUBTY

I'm now sure I follow you, please explain.

PROF. TORTS

Well it's very simple. Each evolving order of things needs/requires new perceptions from the people expected to make that order work.

For about a decade now, we have been involved in the creation of a new world order.

MOTHER EARTH

We? Did I hear you say, we? We have been involved...........isn't that a bit exaggerated?

DOUBTY

Not really! Whether we are conscious of our actions or not, we have been involved.

PROF. TORTS

I agree with you, but I'd say it a bit differently. I'd say whether we are aware of what's happening or not, it's still happening. There are people consciously involved in the process, and there are those who are simply participating. Not consciously mind you.

MOTHER EARTH

And there are the fall outs.

PROF. TORTS

Yea, of course, there are always the fall outs. That's usually occurs because as I said, their participation is in spite of any awareness of what's going on around them.

DOUBTY

And, you call there people, "fall outs"? Why are they fall outs?

MOTHER EARTH

Because there is nothing for them to do. The new system does not offer these people anything, except hardship and suffering or, clerical work, and service jobs.

DOUBTY

Is that because of a lack of preparation?

PROF. TORTS

Yes, neither the new system – i.e. order – or people who suffer are prepared to receive the other.

DOUBTY

You mean the new system is not geared up to handle the new problems that may arise............

PROF. TORTS

........And, the people who are displaced by the changes too drastic, run seeking safety elsewhere, then there are those who become the other classes – sometimes called the underclass, at others, the lower class – meaning inferior.

In fact, they are the victims of change. Whatever else they turn out to be, they are the victims.

DOUBTY

Why are they victims? Or, as you put it, why are they the victims?

MOTHER EARTH

Usually because they are the least informed about what's going on?

DOUBTY

Why are they the least informed?

MOTHER EARTH

Their access to and use of information does not keep them informed about areas of change most likely to have a direct bearing on their future. (Repeat)

DOUBTY

The least informed!

MOTHER EARTH

Also, their level of understanding of the languages they need to know is usually so limited that they can sit and have the most important information broadcast directly to them and not hear a word said. In other words, 90% of the people who read that sentence don't understand it.

DOUBTY

You mean, they don't understand what it means?

PROF. TORTS

Exactly! They've never learned the other purposes of languages. Most of the words they hear they never bother to find out what they mean.

DOUBTY:

Why?

PROF. TORTS

Probably because we live in a tele-video world. We depend more on what we see than what we hear.

DOUBTY

That puts the average Joe at a major disadvantage, doesn't it?

MOTHER EARTH

That's an understatement. No one seems capable of teaching the consuming public how to learn from television. It's there in the stories, and most of the people I know miss the point because they did not critique the stories as literature courses in school. You remember, this line means that!........It was slow, but you learned the way words may be changed around to say the same thing, or something different. Whatever!

PROF. TORTS

And, many people – like the Blacks in America – Lose their birth right in the process.

DOUBTY

That is why we are here?

MOTHER EARTH

That's how we're here.

PEOT SAID

Mirror, mirror on the wall, This is no intentional call, but, now that you are in my sight, was the great move a necessary flight, one that should cause I to lose my birth right?

(To the mirror)

More than a half-a-century has passed, and may your infinite wisdom last. Less than another half to go, before you are a rare breed of the 20ᵗʰ century.

Minus your age, and we guess how long our musicians live. Subtract from the life of a Black musician living in This America, and you'll give how long an African may live, if she's lucky. So, do we count our blessings? Count our dollars?

MOTHER EARTH

Count your dollars. Is that all? IS THAT ALL?

(Pause)

The answer this generation gives will either remove our ancestor's lands from misery, or cause further turmoil and suffering.

(Change moods)

Ruin! As the old folks use to say, "They just ruined it." But, whose fault is it? No fault, any more! Too far gone for that, now. Now we must act. Yes, act like rational intelligent human beings, just once in our lifetime.

Just once! (Pause) (Change)

So we all sat silently, listening while he played the music our souls unleashed. We sat! And, listened! Can you hear? Can you hear?

SMART ASS

Power! That's why the powerful are rich. Money brings them power. Can you imagine owning a ranch that is one million acres big? Illusion? Illusion? Is this really an Illusion? Do I really own 1,000,000 acres of land? Do I really own all that is there? All that is out there?

Is this all? That I own?

POET SAID

Can you hear? Can you hear? Music of the night, beautiful, articulate, proud, lyrical, picturesque. Can you hear? Can you hear? The quiet giant played his music of the night. The crowd looked on/listened with awe.

Awh! Awh! Did you see/ hear him do that? Did you see that? Awh! Awh! We actually dreamed our realities through his horn as he played his music. Did you hear that? (Pause)

Did you hear? Did you hear? Tell me, if you had three wishes, what would you ask for? Now, tell me this, what would you be willing to do to earn you first wish? Remember, you may want to make your last wish first. There are no restrictions here.

CHORUS

What did he say? Did you hear that he said? Did he really say.......

POET SAID

However, whatever you wish you must show the process of obtaining it, and the challenge you expect to receive. Creativity is a premium.

SOLO

But who is the giant? Who is the quiet giant?

CHORUS

it's only '84 and we're already sayin "way back in "77". Do we know what happened way back in "77"?

SOLO

Can you remember?

CHORUS

Do you remember?

SOLO

What did he say when he blew such beautiful music, our music?

CHORUS

What did he say?

SOLO

Can you recall?

CHORUS

It's only '84, and we can't remember '77.

SOLO
Can you hear? Can you hear?

CHORUS
The cry of the people was for the love of peace, they just ruined it. They've ruined it. But, what do we know? What do we know? Another 12 million years to go. What do we do, now? What do we do, now? Just 12 million years to go. But what do we know?

MOTHER EARTH
It was a fall from grace. That's why the Black man has had to suffer so. He turned away from God. God don't like ugly.

Did you hear me, I said God don't like ugly.

Can I get a here, here?

CHORUS
HERE! HERE!

MOHTER EARTH
Hallaujah

CHORUS
What do we know? Ghettos in the ghetto, communities in communities, communities in the ghetto, ghetto in the community. (Repeat)

What do we know? What do we know? What do we know? Another 12 million years to go.

VELDA
And Allah patiently observes us all!

AUTHORITY
We believe in a policy of non-racialism. By that we mean, all members of society are considered equal. Thus we practice non-recognition of the races, so called. People are judged as individuals, not as members of a particular group. Therefore, we see no need for quotas and affirmative action. Everyone here has ;;;

SMART ASS
Although I agree with the sentiment of your statement, I find that I must disagree with your projection of what has happened to us as African American people. I'd be the first to announce that the policies over the last 16 years have caused a devastating effect on the lives of black folks. A fool can see that. But I would not be so bold as to say that it has destroyed us.(Back stage – time pause)

CHORUS
Ghettos in the Ghetto. Communities in the ghetto. Communities in communities. Ghettos in the communities. (Repeat)

SMART ASS
Times is hard! But I wouldn't exactly say that we are defeated.

(Off stage – Time pause)

AUTHORITY

You may be sterilized, but you can't get an abortion on your own.

CHORUS

You may be sterilized, but you can't get an abortion on your own. (Repeat)

(Speaker continues, nothing said.)

SMART ASS

I come from a time when everything was in abundance.

CHORUS

He must have been around during the war.

SOLO

Which war?

CHORUS

Every war! Aren't things in abundance during the war?

SOLO

I don't know? What's a war?

CHORUS

What's a war?

Nothing but a toy.
A silly game of play.
That's a war.
(Acknowledge for first time)

SMART ASS

I come from a time – you can be silly, if you want to – when everything you needed was there. (Off stage – time pause)

CHORUS

Ask nothing of me, and everything will follow. Restrict me and nothing will be yours.

(Speaker continues, nothing said.)

SMART ASS

But, now looks like everything done disappeared. Right in front of our eyes.

(Enters stage)

PROF. TORTS:

You are looking at a new world. Things are different, now. Things have changed. Nothing stays the same. Not anymore. Things change!

MOTHER EARTH

That is true! But I hop you're not trying to rationalize turmoil and suffering. You asked, what is a war?

SOLO

What is a war?

CHORUS

Nothing but a toy.

MOTHER EARTH

Nothing but a toy?

CHORUS

A silly game of ploy.

MOTHER EARTH

A GAME! War is a silly game? Is that your claim? That war is a game?

Do you mean like the Baltimore Orioles and the Dallas Cowboys?

CHORUS

Who has the claim?
The winners of the game.
The winners of the game.
Have the first claim.

MOTHER EARTH

I say there are no winners anymore.

CHORUS

That's your claim! Who says?

MOTHER EARTH

I say! Humanity says! It is not a game. Cowboys and injuns was not a game.

CHORUS

Sure it was. It was a war game.

MOTHER EARTH

I knew you'd finally show your hand. War is not a game. And, if it is to you may God help you.

CHORUS

Then tell me why did ABCBNBC have instant replays of the war in Vietnam? Score: "30,000 Viet Kooks dead, 125,000 wounded over the past week. No American causalities reported." This is the third week no American causalities were reported. The American Team seems to have a win streak going let's all say, "Go Boys". "Wipe um out, and get your asses back home where you belong."

MOTHER EARTH:

So who has the tapes? Where are the tapes? Are they at CBS or NBC or ABC or all networks three? Where are the tapes? Who has the tapes?

FIRST SOLO

What is the value in preserving your grandmother's letters, post cards, greetings, Bibles, furniture, books, scrapbooks, cookbooks, guilts, 78 RPM's, 45's, BLACK POSTCARDS! Black GREETINGS,.......?

SECOND SOLO

What is the value in making and preserving records/tapes by Guitar Slim?

AUDIENCE

Who is Guitar Slim?

FIRST SOLO

What is the value in videotaping the Haitian ART Exhibit at the Brooklyn Museum, a few years ago?

CHORUS

Was it taped? Was it taped?

SECOND SOLO

What is the value of a central audio-visual library service to those who might want to see something cultural, occasionally?

CHORUS

But, where are the tapes? Who has the tapes? Is it the CIA? Or, the Schomburg? The FBI or ERIC U?

CHORUS

Where are the tapes? Who has the tapes?

FIRST SOLO

Are they in the basement of the Smithsonian? On the streets of our lives moving each obstacle one by one, grain by grain.

CHORUS

But where do we find it? Where is it located, our culture!

SECOND SOLO

It is here? Is it there? Is it everywhere? Where is our culture?

CHORUS

Here! Look over there. It's Everywhere. Look to the North. Look to the South.
It's Everywhere. It's Everywhere. Look to the East. Look to the West.
It's Everywhere. It's Everywhere. Look over here. Look over there.
It's Everywhere. It's Everywhere.

(Another Movement)

FIRST SOLO

A flight through reality is sometimes often painful/joyful.

CHORUS

What do you say? What is today?

FIRST SOLO

What do we say? Make the pain go away. Make our pains go away.

SECOND

Give us joy today.

CHORUS

Joy is a painful way. Pain in a joyful way.

FIRST SOLO

I said give us joy today.

CHORUS

Joy in a painful day. Pain not a joyful day.

SECOND SOLO

We need some joy today.

CHORUS

Joy is painful today. Pain in joyful today.

FIRST SOLO

I need some joy today.

CHORUS

Please make our pains to away. Give us some joy each day.

BOTH SOLOS

I need some joy today. Give us our joy today.

CHORUS

Give us some joy each day. We have our joy we pray.

(Repeat)

SMART ASS

Gibran said, "knowledge is life with wings." What he didn't say was for us to accept its value it must be presented by the characters we identify with: A point intuitively understood by those who've read Jonathan Livingston Seagull. So tell me, do we call Bach a contemporary or a disciple of Gibran?

POET SAID

Twinkle, twinkle, twinkle star. How I've searched for you afar. You seemed so near, but where you are, I cannot determine from this star. I searched every night, By starship flight, Only to find you not by sight.

CHORUS

It's outa-sight, it outa-sight, not to be reached by starship flight.

It's outa-sight, it's outa sight, not to be found in a permanent night.

POET SAID

What to do. Since you're all gone. Should I stay here all alone?

CHORUS

All alone, you're all alone when the starship's gone, you're all alone.

POET SAID

12 million years to go. Don't you recall, I said there's only 12 million years to go.

CHORUS

What's 12 million years. For a starship flight. That can be done in a single night. A single night on a starship flight. That can be done at our dream's delight.

POET SAID

I pray you see us through our flight in search of you.

CHORUS

A single night, A perfect night. The only flight, on a perfect night.

POET SAID

I pray that is we fail our souls don't go to hell.

CHORUS

GO TO HELL. GO TO HELL. If you fail.

[Repeat in any

Arrangement you prefer.]

If you fail. If you fail, Go to HELL.

SOLO

Many eons to go for 26 to be no more. Even then 26 will come again.

CHORUS

You are my destiny. Please come and set I free. I am beholden to thee.

Am I your gift to be?

(Mother Earth enters unexpectedly speaking)

MOTHER EARTH

I have no problem with your search to discover. Your need to know, I find it a rather curios way to learn about your vast surroundings, as a matter-a-fact. My question is this, however, why must what you discover always be turned into a commodity for its value to be realized?

Why must wars be fought for you to test its value? Why must the (body/earth) from which you came be subjected to your urge to know how much you can take from it?

Again! Again! Again! And Again!

Why must you subjugate others in order to have a better material life? Is there something you have learned that I don't know! After all, I'm only Mother Earth. I can't possibly know all. Do you know more? Something else, maybe?

As I understand, we arranged things so that life could evolve/ continue from a number of possibilities. As things turned out, you were one of those possibilities: Sort-of-an-unknown.

You were always referred to as the unknown. The more you learned, the more you wanted to know. A rather interesting trait, we thought.

The truly fascinating thing about you was, the more you learned about how things are, the more you wanted to arrange them to meet your desires. I'm sure I don't have to quote any examples to make the point…….

……And, contrary to Western myth you don't abandon your "Man is the center of the universe" thesis at all. You expanded it.

SMART ASS
We may turn out to be nothing but an unsuccessful experiment of intellectual beings operating on a continuum of free will/determinism or as you put it biologically, genetics v. environment. But isn't all the same?

BLOOD
If we fail, maybe the next time humans, or whatever, will be programmed to operate from another set of principles.

SMART ASS
Like the bees and ants?

BLOOD
Yeah! Something like that, wouldn't it be funny if we woke up one morning an all the roaches, bees, wasps, yellow jackets, and water bugs had put a quarantine around all of us.

You know, just like that!

ANT
All right you humans, we're tired of your shit, git off the pot…….don't move 'til we tell you. HA! HA! HA!

BLOOD
(To Audience) Just sit there and think about it for a while. You know what I mean? (Audience laughs) HA! (Now serious) Some how, if we don't find a solution, nature has built-in safeguards to protect itself. That's what I believe.

SMART ASS
Man may very well be on the verge of discovering "the beginning." The true Adam & Eve story, as it were – if I may be "proper" for a moment. He may very well learn how to clone "reproduce" uni-sexually, create an atom, or anything else you can imagine, but if he continues to use warfare as the most productive way

of discovering the value of the atom, he may become an abstraction that is no longer attached to himself objectively or subjectively. In that case, the imagination of man will no longer be necessary because man will have become what he is trying to discover. AN ABSTRACTION! HA! HA!

MOTHER ARLENE

We must always remember that those who make the rules define reality.

(Chorus repeats slowly singing)

STREAMS

We must remember that those who make the rules define reality. Lord. Lord. Lord. Lord. Lord. Lord.

(Response)

I said, Lord. Lord. Lord. Lord. Lord.

MOTHER ARLENE

Is that why training us – I know that this is awkward sounding but I must get it out before I forget my thought. Did you understand my question? Let me repeat it again. Is that why Black people are so slow to accept their own ancestors contributions to world culture? Even when they themselves inadvertently practice that same basic culture? Is that our problem, that is, we don't control our own reality?

STREAMS CHORUS

Lord. Lord. Lord. Lord. Lord. Lord. Lord.

(Response)

I said, Lord. Lord. Lord. Lord. Lord. Lord.

MOTHER ARLENE

Is that because when our reality is defined by someone else, both of us start to believe that only the person who defines, knows all the answers about what, when, and how the beginning happened?

STREAMS

I said, Lord. Lord. Lord. Lord. Lord. Lord.

MOTHER ARLENE

Sure, exactly. Those who solve the mystery of the beginning can claim the knowledge. Such a narrow focus causes the ones with the most technology to claim the most favored position. Through the power of the gun – faith is what they call it –we are made to believe that the claimant has earned exclusive right to the most favored position.

STREAMS

Lord. Lord. Lord. Lord. Lord. Give me faith Lord. I need faith Lord. I need faith.

(Response)

CHORUS

I said, Lord. Lord. Lord. Lord. Lord.

MOTHER ARLENE
(Transforms back into Mother Earth)

Of course when evidence is required, a simple referral to a written document will suffice.

STREAMS
Give me faith Lord. I need faith Lord. Lord. Lord. Lord. I need faith.

(Response)

CHORUS
I said, Lord. Lord. Lord. Lord. Lord. Lord.

MOTHER EARTH
(Mother Earth appears as Mother Arlene again)

….And, those credited with writing the document verifying their claim of the most favored position because they possess the document of verification. After all, they can explain the beginning. They are the beginning.

STREAMS
Through revelation or verification, I need faith. Lord. Lord. Lord. Lord. Lord. Through revelation or verification, I need faith Lord. Give me faith Lord. I said….

MOTHER EARTH
There's, is the true word. The written word, as the keepers of knowledge and information! They are the providers of light, the interpreters of God in the image of man, the god, and the white man. Is that why black people fear their potential?

STREAMS
(Sing) Let me aim high, Lord. Through faith, let me aim high Lord. Give me faith Lord. By revelation or verification give me faith. I need faith Lord. Please, give me faith Lord. Lord. Lord. Lord. Lord.

SMART ASS
Do you remember how a famous athlete publically scolded Paul Robeson, the person responsible for him being in sports? Can you image an athlete chastising Paul?

STREAMS
Give me faith Lord. Please give me faith Lord. I need faith Lord. Please give me faith Lord. Lord. Lord. Lord. Lord.

(Response)

I said, Lord. Lord. Lord. Lord. Lord. Lord. Lord.

DOUBTY
We must remember that those who make the laws define our reality.

STREAMS
Lord. Lord. Lord. Lord. Lord. Lord. I said….

(Call and response)

AUDIENCE

Give me peace. We want peace. Give me peace. We want peace. Give me peace. We want peace.

AUTHORITY

Obviously a rebellion in the making. Ban this work. Ban it now. NOW!

STREAMS

Lord. Lord. Lord. Lord. Lord. Lord. I said....

AUDIENCE

Give me peace. We want peace.

AUTHORITY

These's a rebellion in the making. Banishing it. Banish it. A rebellion is in the making. Banish it. Banish it.

AUDIENCE

Give us peace Lord. Please give us some peace.

AUTHORITY

That's Communism.

STREAMS

Communism. Communism. That's called communism. Communism.

(Response)

I said, Lord. Lord. Lord. Lord. Lord.

AUTHORITY

COMMUNISM. COMMUNISM. ALL OF THAT IS COMMUNISM. WHAT YOU SAY IS COMMUNISM. COMMUNISM.

STREAMS

NO IT'S FASCISM. FASCISM. I SAY FASCISM. FASCISM.

AUDIENCE

LORD. LORD. LORD. LORD. LORD. LORD. I SAID....

POET SAID

Mirror, mirror. Please forgive, but you are my only way out. With you it's revelation and reflection. With you, I can see myself.

MIRROR

Reflect!

STREAMS

Reflections reveal the object itself.

(Response)

Reflections reveal the subject as self.

AUDIENCE

In the year 2020 the meek shall inherit the earth.

(End simultaneously)(Build up to a soulful searching crescendo)

AUDIENCE/STREAMS

Lord. Lord. Lord. Lord. Lord. Lord.

(Hands are clapping. Body language shows spiritual up-lift-ment. But not a carnival.)

(Streams become background music to Smart Ass.)

SMART ASS

You want to know what the vote for Jesse's all about? (Pause) We look around, and what do we see? Everybody who was ahead of is moved up a notch or two after we made our demands for human rights in the 50's and 60's. And, we still got high unemployment, low paying jobs, bad health, poor education, and not shelter.

So, we say, if we have to we go to alone. It's really easy. We already vote as a block. Always have. All we need is to do now is increase the numbers.

We want Jesse. We want Jesse. If we don't win, we understand that. The point is, we don't loose. If we keep sticking together. Everything will be okay.

(Solo singer for Streams is pacing around stage in a sort of rhythmic fashion.)

STREAMS

(Sing) Don't we say, everything's okay.

(Response)

CHORUS

When it goes my way, everything's okay. Everything's okay when it goes my way.

(Fade off the stage) (Enters Moderator)

MODERATOR

WELL!

AUDIENCE

WELL!

(Great laughter of relief comes from the audience.)

MODERATOR

Well, obviously this is not what we had planned. This was not our planned format for the evening. Although it got dramatic for a while I hope it has cleared the air for us to move forward.

As you know, we began with a talk on learning by Professor Torts. Actually, we started with a poem by Mr. Said Saud. In any case, Professor Torts lecture on learning somehow led us into a rather spirited debate on a topic I have given a great deal of thought to: Birth rights.

Simply to repeat matters, I read a quote from Mr. Spencer-Brown the noted mathematician which said, "There can be no distinction without motive; and there can be no motive unless contents are seen to differ in value."

BLOOD

The question is, what are we going to do about it? Our right are violated; and like mother nature said....

AUDIENCE

MOTHER EARTH. MOTHER ARLENE. IT'S MOTHER EARTH.

BLOOD

Whatever! Anyway, remember Rockefeller at Attica?Ain't no way to justify (audience becomes uneasy with that reminder.)Ain't no way to justify killing all those bloods, and the guards too. Ain't no way in my book. These dudes in prison, where they goin' to? Huh? Where they goin' to. Tell me that. Like I said, know what the problem is**. What we gon' do 'bout it.

MOTHER ARLENE

Calm down. Calm down.

AUDIENCE

Chill out.

MOTHER ARLENE

Yea, chill out. As the young bloods like to say.

YOUNG BLOOD

Use to say. That's old.

MOTHER ARLENE

What's the latest?

BLOOD

Back to the same. You know, "cool it mother."

YOUNG BLOOD

HE DON'T KNOW WHAT HE'S TALKIN' ABOUT. (slap five and laugh)

MOTHER EARTH

WELL ANYWAY, I'M SURE THAT MY POINT WAS (voice lowers) understood just as well. Now, what were you saying Blood?

BLOOD

Oh! I'm through. I was finished.

MOTHER EARTH

Okay. Mr. Moderator. You were asking your question again. I believe we are still trying to understand birth rights as a principle. Is that correct?

MODERATOR
Yes, that is correct. I could not have said it any better. Not trying to be – auh! Where did you people come from? You have so much life. Energy.

Determination.

MOTHER EARTH
Sir, I suggest that you quit while you are running ahead.

MODERATOR
Yes. I agree. Anyway my question was....

(Audience laughs)

....What is the basis for defining any given property or thing as having more value than another?

(Audience looks at each other in puzzlement.)

Is the amount of activity it tends to generate? The space it occupies?

(Audience still does not know what Moderator is asking.)

What is the basis for a particular class of individuals assuming the most favored position?

What distinguishes them from others, birthright? Heritage? Name?

MOTHER EARTH
Name? What name?

MODERATOR
Like the Puritans! The founding fathers.

(Call)

STREAMS:
What 's in a name?

(Response)

The basis of a claim.

(Call)

The basis of a claim?

(Response)

That's what's in a name.

MODERATOR
George Washington! Abe Lincoln!

STREAMS
Birds of a feather flock together.

MODERATOR

Aren't those the names that made us free?

AUDIENCE

What's in a name?

STREAMS

Birds of a feather flock together.

AUDIENCE

The basis of our claim.

STREAMS

Birds of a feather flock together.

AUDIENCE

Is that why our name?

BLOOD

Are you trying to tell me that there was no revolutionary Black during the colonial wars of the Americas? Not even in these United States called America? Not even one?

STREAMS

Birds of a feather flock together.

AUDIENCE

What's in a name?

STREAMS

Birds of a feather flock together.

AUDIENCE

The basis of a claim.

STREAMS

Birds of a feather flock together.

AUDIENCE

The basis of a claim.

STREAMS

Birds of a feather flock together.

AUDIENCE

That's what's in a name.

STREAMS

Birds of a feather flock together.

MODERATOR

To answer your question, "what distinguishes the most favored from the rest of us," I'd like to quote from Mr. Spencer-Brown's Laws of Form. On page one, he said, "If a content is of value a name can be taken to indicate this value." Thus, the calling of the name can be identified with the value of the content.

BLOOD

So the name "Puritan" automatically gives that person the most favored position in America. Is that your point? So, who runs America? The Puritans.

MODERATOR

Yes, exactly! Obviously, the Puritans – or Pilgrams if you must – are valued more highly than other Americans, and that value can be identified with the calling of that name: Puritan.

STREAMS

"We take as given the idea of distinction and the idea of indication, and that we cannot make an indication without drawing a distinction. We take, therefore, the form of distinction for the form." (This passage is repeated over and over. At first slowly, with an increase in the pace as the repetition continues.)

(The Disunity Ensemble joins in repeating the same passage but with a different meaning intended. As they join in, it is a counter to the Streams repetition. Both are now repeating the same passage at counter time with different meanings. Antagonism runs high until it ends with both repeating the passage at the same time.)

(Streams chorus breaks out into a counter statement.)

CHORUS

IL-LUS-SION! IL-LUS-SION! IL-LUS-SION! IL-LUS-SION!

DISUNITY EMSEMBLE

You must indicate. Is that the motive? You must indicate. Is that the motive?

LEAD SINGER

With junk that we don't need. And, pills that make us bleed, we say,.....

CHORUS

Everything is okay. Everything is okay.

LEAD SINGER

I said with junk that makes us bleed and pills we don't need we say.....

CHORUS

Everything is okay. Everything is okay.

LEAD SINGER

Don't we say.....

CHORUS

Everything is okay. Everything is okay.

(Woman screams from audience)

LEAD SINGER

I said with junk that we don't need pills that make us bleed, we say….

CHORUS

Everything is okay. Everything is okay.

LEAD SINGER

Remember this is 1984, we've got 12 million years to go.

CHORUS

Everything is okay. Everything is okay. (Repeat sequence)

LEAD SINGER

Remember this is 1984 and 26 million is now 34. Yet we say….

CHORUS

Everything is okay.   Everything is okay. (repeat sequence)

LEAD SINGER

Do we now have another 8 befo we count the 12 we had befo.

CHORUS

Everything is okay. Everything is okay. It's only 1984 so what do we know? Another 12 million before 1 million years of atomic snow. One million years of atomic rain showers befo another 26 million years in a row.

LITTLE WONDER

Okay, I give up.

POET SAID

What do you mean, you give up? Give up what? Oh, you're talking about the poem….

AUDIENCE

The poem? I'm talking about the whole affair. The whole damn thing.

POET SAID

…The poem about 12 million years to go. You know what that's about. —I'm really referring to the last one. It was an explanation of the first one I recited. HERE NOW AND THERE. Scientists say that the earth goes through a radical transformation every 26 million years. I think it begins with 1 million years of radiation showers, then earth begins the reconstruction process again. Or, something like that. I ain't no scientist, so I might have the facts wrong. You must admit that it is an interesting theory.

LITTLE WONDER

FOR ANOTHER 26 MILLION YEARS? Oh, sorry.   I didn't know that I was talking so loud. (Audience laughs, but watches this little wonder with interest.)

POET SAID

Yes! But what do we know? In '77 we had 26 million poor but now it's 84, and we have 34. But what do we know? Where do we do?

LITTLE WONDER
So, where does the number 12 come from?

POET SAID
I think it was some astro-physicists who said that 14 million years have passed, and we have 12 million to go.

AUDIENCE
So how are we suppose to know any of this? What are you sayin?

(Another member of audience shouts out, "Public radio. Magazines.")

AUDIENCE
So how do you do it?

POET SAID
Do what?

AUDIENCE
Use poetry to say what I ain't never heard before. How do you do that?

POET SAID
You know. This is 1984 with the final battle to go. So beware. Prepare with econofare. For the final battle on T.V. on NBC, May 6,7,8, 1984. Prime time.

STREAMS
MAY DAY! MAY DAY! Prepare for the final battle in living color brought to you by the sponsors of the 1984 Olympics in Los Angeles, California, U.S.A. MAY DAY! MAY DAY! Prepare for the final battle. MAY DAY! MAY DAY! (Repeat)

POET SAID
With only 12 years to go and 26 million now 34 and the final battle in 84 although we have another 8 before we count the 12 we have to go. What do we know? What do we know? It's now 1984 But what do we know. Another 12 before 1 million years of radiation showers 1 million years of radiation showers. Before another 26 million in a row. So what do we do, now? In '77 we had 26 million po Now it's 34 in 84 So what do we do, now? What do we know?

STREAMS
(Begin singing) Everything is okay. (Repeat in a funcky spiritual blues vain)

LEAD SINGER
With junk we don't need. With pills that make us bleed. If we don't take heed, can we say? Everything is okay? Can we say....

CHORUS
Give me peace. We want peace. (Repeat)

RESPONSE
LORD! LORD! LORD! LORD! LORD! I SAID.....

(Streams become quiet as a new speaker stands to say his peace)

JAZZ MUSICIAN

You know, I really had not planned to delve into this matter of birth-right – especially as it relates to Black music – because it is so personal to our artists, so very personal to me as a musician. To put it bluntly, I must go to some where else simply to hear my music on record. You know what I mean? Simply to know my contributions I must purchase my music as a commodity.

ANNOYN

A good! It's called a good. What you purchased is either a good or a service. This commodity operates – is presented – as a good, service or entertainment. Which ever one you want you must purchase for a price. The question is where is the value of the product found? In it's creation? How is that determined?

These esoteric questions seem to bother me. This can take us so far away from what we are trying to learn, that I get disturbed when I hear one beingraised.

(Audience looks at Annoying in disbelief)

JAZZ MUSICIAN

Oh, I agree totally. That's why I've tried to remain silent. You see, it's esoteric to other people. For me it's basic. Do I, or do, I not have a right to have immediate access to my creation as a commodity without having a mortgage placed on my past?

ANNOYIN

You mean, future.

JAZZ MUSICIAN

I mean past.

ANNOYN

So what is your question? I don't quite understand you.

(Audience laughs, "Is she serious?")

JAZZ MUSICIAN

My question is this. Do I have a right to preserve the music I created?

ANNOYN

Right? I'm not sure I can accept the word right as you are using it. "Privilege seems to be better suited for what you are talking about.

JAZZ MUSICIAN

Privilege? What privilege? What's privilege? An assumed right. Okay, privilege. Whatever. In that case, I so have the right to take the privilege and record what I create.

ANNOYN

No! You do not know?

JAZZ MUSICIAN
Then who does?

ANNOYN
It's rather complex.

JAZZ MUSICIAN
In what way? Complex in what way? Does the musician not have a right to have his or her music heard? Should there not be facilities to house our musicians so that they may work/ play their art and more than occasionally.

BOTHSIDES
…If they so desire. They may not want to sing or perform often. Or, have their music recorded.

JAZZ MUSICIAN
I agree. Whatever the arrangement might be, it should be designed to encourage creativity; and the preservation of our culture.

(Accepting J. M.'s thoughts. Both sides move the discussion further.)

BOTHSIDES
A musician should not have to wait until everyone goes to work during the day so that he can practice his instrument.

AUDIENCE: There are women musicians, too.

BOTHSIDES
Sorry about that. Arrangements might be made with public schools allowing the musicians to rehearse in their spaces if they will offer something in return like music lessons for a fee, of course. They might organize lab bands,… you know public service and creativity. Become a teacher.

(Member of audience tries to start a jingle only to have the rest boo her down.)

BOO BOO
Damn, can't even be creative around here.

(Audience laughs)

(Someone in the audience orders everyone to be silent. Old Lady enters stage.)

OLD LADY
Keep on playin'

AUDIENCE
What did she say?

OLD LADY
I said, keep on playin'. As long as you keep in playin' they can't take nothin' from you.

(Facing audience front and center)

Did you hear what I said? Yawl Thank you know everything nowadays.   Don't you. You betta listen to me. You can't discount us simply because we's ole. (Old Lady moves slowly across stage as she speaks.) Wisdom! When knowledge is old wisdom is told. (Pause) Yawl Betta pay attention to the signs; read the Good Book; listen to Dr. King. He died for our sins. Don't let....

(Streams quietly assemble behind her)

(Verse)

STREAMS:

Our sins be his death in vain
he died for our sins
will we sin our sins again
or will we sin another sin
for our profits to die again

(Chorus)

Will our sins again be that sin
Will we sin that sin again

(Verse)

He died for our sins
Will we sin again and again
Will our sins again be that sin
Will we sin that sin again
Or will we sin another sin
For our prophets to die again.

(Chorus)

Will our sins again be that sin
Will we sin that sin again

(Verse)

If the king died for our sins
And yet we sin again
Will our sins contain that sin
Or will it be another sin
that take our prophets lives again

(Chorus)

Will our sins again be that sin
Will we sin that sin again
Will our prophets die as revenge
Because we committed anther fated sin

JAZZ MUSICIAN

Is our sin – that fatal sin – our failure to protect the birth right? Our culture – at times – can be so oppressive. At other times, we can appear so laid back; unconcerned about any thing, even those things that happen to us. We seem so unconcerned when our masters die.

BOTHSIDES

Yes, but what can we do about it? There's really nothing we can do.

JAZZ MUSICIAN

Except sin. Is that your point?

BOTHSIDES

The point is we don't have any real power in this society. None of us. Wouldn't you agree?

AUDIENCE

I agree.

GOFER

Well I don't. We have as much power as we choose to use.

AUDIENCE

Easier said than done.

BOTHSIDES

Yes, darn near impossible.

DOUBTY

The man ain't giving up shit. Not without a fight. He didn't rob and steal from everybody else because he planned to build a new land of milk and honey for everybody.

BLOOD

Damn sure didn't.

GOFER

I know! I know that. So, are you proposing that we lay down and die like hogs. Give up? Is that all we have to do? Completely give up?

BOTHSIDES

I didn't say that.

DOUBT:

Neither did I.

GOFER

Then what was your point?

(Old Lady enters stage again.   Unexpectedly)

OLD LADY

SIMPLETONS! DON'T YOU CHILLUNS KNOW THAT IF YOU DON'T PRESERVE

YOUR OWN CULTURE, YOU GIVE UP YOUR RIGHTS TO EVERYTHING?

(Pause) Don't yawl know that? (Complains as she leaves stage) Yawl don't never give up. Heritage. That's all yawl gots. And , it ain't got nothin' to do with you being Black. (Turns around – heads back.) You ain't po' 'cause you Black. You po' 'cause the white man don't care nothin' 'bout nobody 'cept hisself. He wanna spend his time scheme-ing on how he's gon' make his next kill. (Decides to return to center stage.) Then have the nerve to tell us he's doin' us a favor. Donin's us a favor.

(Disunity Ensemble takes up chant)

DISUNITY ENSEMBLE

Create a new skill

On how to kill
Make the next kill
The best kill.

STREAMS

Give us peace. We want peace.
Give us peace. We want peace.

DISUNITY ENSEMBLE

Create a new skill
On how to kill
Make the next kill
A death kill.

STREAMS

Give us peace. We want peace.
Give us peace. We want peace.

FAITHFUL RADICAL

Biological warfare! Chemical warfare! Nuclear warfare.
What is it all for 'cept to kill.

STREAMS

Give us peace. We want peace.
Give us peace. We want peace.

DISUNITY EMSEMBLE

Create a new skill
On how to kill
Make the next kill
The final kill.

STREAMS

Give us peace. We want peace.
Give us peace. We want peace.

JAZZ MUSICIAN

Well, what's the point? Is it that our birth-right is not important enough to hold onto? Can you give up what you are born with without paying a heavy price? Can you do that without a heavy penalty? Can you do that without a heavy penalty being inflicted? On the individual and group simultaneously? I'll give you an example. Red Garland joined our ancestors the other day.

BOTHSIDES

What was that?

BLOOD

Red Garland is dead?

SMART ASS:

No he's not! He is? When did….?

BOTHSIDES

….Whose Red Garland?

JAZZ MUSICIAN

He passed on into the other world the other day in Dallas.

SMART ASS

Red Garland is a Jazz pianist whose greatest fame came while playing with Miles Davis.

JAZZ MUSICIAN

That was a very famous Jazz group at the time.

SMART ASS

The Miles Davis Quintet

BLOOD

Quartet, too.

DOUBTY

I've heard of Miles Davis, but never anything about, what's his name.

JAZZ MUSICIAN

Red Garland.

BLOOD

He died the other day.

JAZZ MUSICIAN

He's not dead. Hr lives in Dallas, Texas. The Masters of our music can't die. They live on in their music. Our music. They may move onto the beyond, but they don't….unless.

BOTHSIDES:Don't what?They don't do what? Unless.

JAZZ MUSICIAN

…Don't record it., their is always that possibility that their works were never recorded. That is virtually a sin.

SMART ASS

You didn't say "die." She was listening for die.

JAZZ MUSICIAN

Thanks! "Die" unless we don't support them. There don't seem to be many roles for accomplished musicians any more.

BLOOD

Yea, it can get very lonely to you if nobody is listening to you when you're playin'. Kinda lonely out there in the beyond.

(Old lady enter front and center. Other actors move to the background.)

OLD LADY

Only a fool travels down blind's alley. Only those who don't know where their nakedness is seek protection from the clothin' of the flesh. Only those who become stagnant in their culture loose their birth-right. (Exit)

(Streams begin to chant in a loud whisper that is echoed.)

STREAMS

What was that? What was that? What was that? What was that?

(Return to discussion on birth-rights.)

SMART ASS

As I was saying, the death – or as Gofer said, "travel in to the beyond" – of Red Garland only points out how it is so easy for our musicians to enter the unknown simply by us forgetting the past without being dead.

FAITHFUL RADICAL

So he leaves behind the past. Leaving none of the present?

JAZZ MUSICIAN

No. No. We do that! The musician – Jazz/ Classical – musician remembers the past. Completes the circle. We forget to teach our offspring what it's all about. By the way Red Garland is not dead. He lives in Dallas, Texas.

(Poet enters)

POET SAID

Why is it so easy for our musicians to enter the unknown? While, they leave behind all that is past? Yet, leaving none of what they left present in our consciousness. (Pause. Reflection) But it is only those who make that trip through the unknown who seem to reach immorality – in the beyond.

(Streams begin to chant in a loud whisper with echo.)

STREAMS

Is that so? Is that so? Is that so? Is that so?

LEAD SINGER
Is it so that those who travel through the unknown reach immorality in the beyond? So, what happens to the rest?

CHORUS
Of us? What's suppose to happen to the rest of us?

OLD LADY
Chil-lun remember only those who occupy the most favored position can claim control over all other's birth rights. They make the laws. Is that a lie? Caught you? (Pause) Didn't I ? if we believe that the only way we can git ahead is to act like those folks who have kept us down, then ain't nothin' good ever gon' happen to us. We'll always be left outta everything. Ain't nothin' good kin ever happen like that. You gotta believe in your self. If you ever gon' do anything in life, you gotta believe in yourself. Ain't no two ways 'bout it.

DOUBTY
Well? What are we suppose to do? What's goin to happen to us?

AUDIENCE
Well? What are we suppose to do? What's goin to happen to us?

AUDIENCE
PRAY! (Laughter)

MODERATOR
We'd better listen to Old Lady. What's she's telling us is basically true, you know! She completes the circle for us.

DOUBTY
What do you mean?

MODERATOR
You know? She pointed out so clearly how we indicate differences between each other. How we make distinctions.

FAITHFUL RADICAL
So did Mother Earth! She also said she is not taking any more of our self-destruction urges. She said she's tired.

BLOOD
Yea, what about caretaker? He rapped some heavy stuff too. You know! Came outta a whole different bag. Where'd he get that stuff from?

SMART ASS
And don't forget Blood. I didn't know the dude had it in 'em. That thing he did on Mingus was…Phew!

(Slap five)

DOUBTY
Yea, what was that joke he made about those insects?

SMART ASS

Oh yea! Something about, "we tired 'o yowl shit, git off de pot."

(Laughter—Slap five)

FAITHFUL RADICAL

….And, what about the Professor, Dr. Torts. He made some good points, too..

(Someone in background)

AUDIENCE

…Always gotta have some liberal mudda fudda come talkin' some shit.

FAITHFUL RADICAL

Don't run that mess on me. What is right is right. Somebody's got to say it. And if my memory serves me correctly, if the poet had not led off with his poem you would have been up manure creek without a paddle.

(Pause. Reflection)

So, there is no need to be biased here.

AUDIENCE

RIGHT ON! Manure Creek?

(Professor Torts assumes podium)

PROF. TORTS

I'd like to thank all of you for such a stimulating evening. It was most fascinating. One I shall never forget. I also hope that I might have left some food for thought regarding learning as a process; and, what ever else I might have un-expectantly said. I enjoyed your "sit-in" you were quit a challenge.

ABDUL HAQMED

I know that some of you ain't gonne like it, but I gonna say it anyway. (Pause) what happened here tonight shows what can happen when you become "active" "stick together" "get involved." Brother and sisters.

I don't care what nobody say, if we hadn't showed up things never would have turned out the way it did. As it turned out, a lot of issues got thrown out on the table. Things I most of never thought of before. I know I ain't never heard anything like that before in my life, except my great grand mother use to talk like that.

And, Mother Earth! Man! I don't know, where she came from…Phew! That was some heavy rap. In other words, the only reason tonight happened is we were here.

IMPATIENT

All right! We got the point. Let's go. I'm tired. I gots to work tomorrow.

ABDUL HAQMED

Come on, gimme a break.

POET SAID

As yawl get up to go home, I'd like to leave you with one last thought. You don't have to stop moving. But you have to listen. So, please listen.

AUDIENCE
SHHHHHH! SHHHHHH! Be quiet! Poet Said is about to say something. Go ahead Saa-eed.

POET SAID
Thank you, Brotherman, Sister woman!

Where you are
There might be a star
Whose light mightn't go far?
Not because it is not a star
Whose light can't shine far?
Is it because what you are?
Is who you are?
Do you think that what happened before?
Won't happen again? Think about it.

STREAMS
(In a repetitive manner.) Think about it. I say, Think about it. Think about it. What happened before will happen no more not as before not any more.

What happened before will be no more as it happened before not any more.

CHORUS
Let's draw a ring around a circle. Add in a cross. What do you see? Give it a name. Give it a claim. It's nothing but a game. Ain't nothing a game. Cause each is worth the same.

Each is the same. Ain't nothin' but a game.

(Audience begins leaving while singing is in progress. As chorus is completed, two citizens have a last word before they depart.)

CITIZEN I
You know, no one would think of us as people with a consciousness.

CITIZEN II
Yea, but you can't overstate that point. You're right. We do have a consciousness about us. Our feelings about each other are so mixed-up and confusing, however.

CITIZEN I
What do you mean?

CITIZEN II
Well, take tonight. If we hadn't been standing outside discussing politics, we never would have come to this lecture tonight. Never would we have heard the American Indians....

CITIZEN I
NATIVE AMERICAN! Indigenous Peoples!

CITIZEN II

Native people to the western hemisphere, what ever. Anyway, I never would have thought about them, not the way that Caretaker talked about them tonight. Would you?

CITIZEN I

No not really.

CITIZEN II

But our feelings are so shallow. We talk about the spiritual, but we don't seem to be able to transcend the physical and emotional parts of our lives.

CITIZEN I

I don't understand. And, it's getting late. What's your point? I got to go to work tomorrow.

CITIZEN II

I don't want to take up any more of your time, I know you're busy. Some other time, maybe.

CITIZEN I

NO! NO! Go ahead. I want to hear what you're saying.

CITIZEN II

We have the great distinction of calling ourselves people, how do you say it, people with a consciousness.

CITIZEN I

Being of consciousness.

CITIZEN II

Yes, that's it. Yet we -- our feelings -- at our highest level of consciousness – have only experienced "living" on the physical and emotional plane. We are still unable to consciously enter other worlds without subjecting them to our narrow understanding of things and happenings. We are unable to stop for a moment and say, what does this world contain? You know what I mean?

CITIZEN I

Yes, I know, but that moderator said, we must make a distinction before we can identify – indicate – what it is we saw. Is that your point?

CITIZEN II

That's the point! We must always draw a distinction before we can indicate what we saw. So we go into a foreign culture, make our distinctions, and come out with a wrong interpretation of what we saw. That's such a contradiction.

CITIZEN I

OKAY. I understand. Now, I gotta go. See you later.

CITIZEN II

Yea, later. Thanks for listening.

The end

References

Alinsky, Saul, Twelve (12) rules for Radicals.

Butler, Octavia E. 1979. Kindred. Boston: Bea0con.

Chase-Riboud, Baraba.1979. Sally Hemings. (A Novel). Chicago: Chicago Review Press 2009.

Cox, Oliver Cromwell, 1970 Caste, Class, and Race: A Study in Social Dynamics. New York: Monthly Review Press.

Craig, William James. (Editor) 1916. The Complete Works of William Shakespeare. (Arranged by Henry M. Piironen).

De Tocquevilie, Alexis..(Trans Henry Reeve). Democracy in America.

Du Bois, W.E.B. 1909. The Souls of Black Folk. New York: Dover Publications, Inc, . 1896. The Suppression of the African Slave Trade to the United States 1638-1870. New York Longmans, Greek, and Co.

Dunbar-Ortiz, Roxanne. An Indigenous Peoples History of the United States. ReVisioning America History.

Engels, Fredrich. 1888. The Communist Manifesto [English edition, edited by Fredrich Engels] Fanon, Franc [trans. Richard Philcox]. 1967. Black Skin White Masks. New York: Grove Press. 1963. The Wretched of the Earth. New York: Drove Press.

Fazal, Tanisha M. 2007. State Death: The Politics and Geography of Conquest, Occupation, and Annexation. Princeton: Princeton University Press.

Handsberry, Loraine. 1958. A Raison in three Sun. New York: Random House

Henry, Winston, 1973. Strategy for a Black Agenda. New York: International Publishers.

James, C.L.R. 1963. The Black Jacobins. Vintage Books.

Kwame, Nkrumah. Neo-Colonialism, the Last Stage of Imperialism. ISBN-13: 978-0717801404. ISBN-10: 0717801403

Lynch, Willie. The Willie Lynch Letter and the Making of a Slave. [A Fiction] Marx, Karl. Das Capital.

Machivelli, Niccolo. 1469-1527. 1982. The Prince. Dover Publications, Inc.

Myrdal Gunnar. 1944. An American Dilemma, Harper Books.

Northup. Solomon. 1854. Twelve Years A Slave. Auburn: Derby and Miller.

Orwell, George. 1945. Animal Farm. New York: Harcourt.

Orwell, George. 1949. 1964. New York: Harcourt.

Rodney, Walter, 1972 (2011. How Europe Underdeveloped Africa.

Baltimore: Black Classic Press

Silman, IM Jerry. 1998. The Complete Book of Chess Strategy:

Grandmaster Techniques from A to Z. Los Angeles: Siles Press.

Smith, Adam. 2015. An Inquiry into the Nature and Causes of the Wealth of Nations. Irvine, CA: Xist Publishing.

Sunzi.

Spencer-Brown, G., 1979. Laws of Form.

Stowe, Harriet Beecher. Uncle Tom's Cabin or Life Among The Lowly. A Public Domain Book.

Wagner, Sally. 2001. Roesch. Sisters in Spirit: Haudeenosaunee (Iroquois) Influence on Early American Feminists. Summertown, Inn: Native Voices.

Williams, Eric. 1844 (2015). Capitalism and Slavery. Philadelphia: The Great Library Collection.

Woodson, Carter Godwin. 2010. The Mis-Education of the Negro. Seven Treasures Publications.

www.ingramcontent.com/pod-product-compliance
Lightning Source LLC
Chambersburg PA
CBHW080841120626
46553CB00009B/2519